A
Taste of
Milk & Honey

A
Taste of
Milk & Honey

Fred B. Craddock

ISBN 978-0-9897302-1-1
PRINTED IN THE UNITED STATES OF AMERICA

Stories collected by Beth Roberts and other members of
The Craddock Center Board.

Cover photograph copyright ©2012 by Edd Fuller

First edition
Georgia Mountain Publishing Company
Suches, Georgia
www.georgiamountainpublishing.com

Dedication

To the Children of The Craddock Center

Contents

Foreword

Like legions of others, I am a great fan of Fred Craddock. But the words *fan* or *admirer* do not adequately convey what I feel about Fred. It is more like gratitude, indebtedness. For Fred has offered to us all a fresh way of hearing the gospel: more invitation and less demand, more joy and less moralism, more story—yes, parable—and less instruction. It is not too much to say that over several decades Fred has virtually reshaped the American pulpit. People flock to hear him, sign up in droves for his workshops, avidly await any publication of his.

That's why this volume of his articles, which first appeared in The Craddock Center newsletter, *Milk & Honey*, is so welcome. They are quintessentially Craddock—brief (hardly ever more than 300 words), personal, evocative of a specific situation or issue, and suggestive, leaving us to ponder implications of what has been portrayed. Fred's style proves the maxim, "Great writers are effective because they deal in particulars." The particulars in this case have to do with the ministry of The Craddock Center, which serves the children of that North Georgia mountain area. Fred is passionate about this, and his deep commitment is evident in all he says in these pages. This is the gospel in action. But even here, he avoids the guilt trap. In deft strokes he invites us to share with him what he sees and how he feels, enabling us to picture in our minds what an appropriate response might be.

And how appealing that invitation is. As he reminds us, his vision for the Center is to offer some joy to the children's lives amidst the drudge of need, something to anticipate that brings delight. But because their world so often is one of broken promises, the Center is there to keep its word, rekindle trust, and bring back a sparkle to their eyes.

As Fred is fond of saying, participation in this ministry might just bring a sparkle to our eyes as well. And he adds, who can resist?

—James T. Laney, President Emeritus, Emory University

Introduction

Why Fred Craddock (Almost) Set Up
a Roadside Peanut Stand: The Vision

Have you ever seen one of those street musicians who is playing many instruments at once, engaging hands, feet, and mouth? In the early days of The Craddock Center, Fred Craddock must have looked like one of those performers, using his multiple gifts to bring about the Center that he and Nettie envisioned. In addition to administering the Center, raising money, visiting with children, and building a community, he wrote all of the Center's monthly newsletters, *Milk & Honey*, from which the stories in this book are drawn.

Even as he explained the Center's vision, made appeals for funds, and oversaw the day-to-day operations of the Center, stories were woven throughout everything he said and did. A master storyteller is who he is. In those early days, *Milk & Honey*'s articles focused on the needs and vision of the Center, but the storyteller's voice is heard in every piece he wrote.

From the beginning, the Center has dedicated most of its resources to providing programs that align with its mission, "enriching lives through service." But as folks began to flock to the Center with their needs and dreams and programs expanded, it seemed wise to hire first a part-time, and then a full-time, Executive Director. At that point, the "business of the Center" pieces could be written by the Executive Director, and Dr. Craddock could write stories that inspire and support the work of the Center.

Thus, the first stories in this book will tell you how the vision of Fred and Nettie Craddock became a reality. The later selections allow you to enjoy the deep truths that are always found in the stories of a master storyteller.

If you don't know Fred Craddock personally, you'll meet him in this book. Oh, and if you want to know why Fred Craddock (almost) set up a roadside peanut stand, read on. It's a great story!

—Beth Roberts, Editor

2004

(February)

?? MILK & HONEY ?? OK, so *Milk & Honey* is a bit unusual as the title for the newsletter of The Craddock Center. It's not that I have anything against titles such as *Herald, Messenger, FYI, Courier,* or *Report.* Those are quite acceptable: clear, straightforward, free of puzzlement. However, this monthly piece will be more than a report or journal. Rather, every issue will attempt to remind the reader who we are, what we are attempting, and the vision before us. In ways direct and indirect, we will always center on our purpose as stated on the logo: "enriching lives through service." Our aim is to lift lives above barely getting by; to add some joy, relief, and pleasure, to enlarge sympathy, understanding, and aspiration.

And so, *Milk & Honey.* The image is biblical. To a people in slavery, God promised "a land flowing with milk and honey." To a people wandering in a desert, the promise was of "a land flowing with milk and honey." To a people exiled, marginalized, and without place or power, the promise was "a land flowing with milk and honey."

I love the image; I believe the promise. I hope you do.

MY VISION . . . My vision for The Craddock Center is clear and firm: that we keep our pledge, in some way, every day, to enrich lives through service.

This means that all who work in and through the Center, paid and volunteer, infuse every act and word with the grace of God. This is achieved not by an abundance of religious talk but by being gracious as God is. To be gracious is to welcome all without distinction. Some have and some do not; we make no distinction. Some give and some receive; we make no distinction. Some have been here for generations and some arrived yesterday; we make no distinction. Some are young and some are old; we make no distinction. And every one of us has been, is, or will be a minority person, so who would presume to make distinctions?

To build such a community is difficult but not impossible. It takes time and effort to build trust so that those who have known only isolation or rejection will accept hospitality. Some are so needy that they have not realized what or how much they have to give to others. A few come running but many must be sought, and none are to be forgotten.

The program of the Center is determined by need. In some cases it may begin with food, clothing, or housing, but that is only the beginning. There is no commandment, "Thou shalt barely get by." Every life needs enrichment and that means classes in health care, job training, family economics, child-rearing. It means music and art and storytelling. It means getting together to listen to each other's stories and to enjoy one another. It means to include the confined, by visits, cards, calls, and gifts. It is to say, "This is a good place to live, to raise a family, to build friendships, to grow old, and to die." This is my vision, and to it I give my life.

WHAT WILL PROBABLY HAPPEN at the Center Board meeting on March 2nd is this: the Board will enthusiastically embrace the idea of purchasing a van or bus to be customized for books and storytelling and songs, to be painted children's colors and designs, to have a special horn or bell, to be driven to schools, parks, trailer parks, country roads, anywhere, everywhere, taking stories, books, and songs to children; and people who read this will want to help pay for the vehicle and buy books, and volunteer to help decorate it and drive it, and Miss Betsy and Miss Pam will want to have a contest among the

800 three- and four-year-olds we serve to choose a name for the vehicle, and . . . what else?

That's probably what will happen.

(March)

O, THE BURDEN OF THE PROPHET! I never knew until recently how heavy is the burden of the prophet. In the February issue of *Milk & Honey*, I made a prediction; it has come true, and now I am besieged by folk wanting their fortunes told and tips on races.

I predicted that the Center Board would enthusiastically support the purchase of a commercial vehicle to be customized, painted brightly, filled with children's books, and commissioned to take books, storytellers, and singers to every place in the area where there are children.

I also predicted that many folk would want to help with this slightly expensive project. This prediction will come true soon, and it will happen, as the Bible says, "on this wise." From now until April 15, gifts of any amount will be welcomed; we prefer many smaller gifts to a few large ones. Mark your check for the "Story Express." If it should happen that on April 15 we are a few dollars short of the $35,000 we need, then I will bring this shortfall to the attention of a few friends who apparently had not heard this appeal.

Will we get this vehicle? Yes, even if I have to set up a roadside stand and sell boiled peanuts and fish bait, do a bit of motorcycle repair, and dabble in acupuncture.

Giving to this program will make you happy.

(April)

BOILED PEANUTS, ANYONE? Are we still on track to purchase a commercial vehicle to be customized, painted brightly, filled with children's books, and commissioned to take books, singers, and storytellers to every place in the area where there are children?

3

You better believe it! The word is spreading and interest is growing, wherever *Milk & Honey* is read, wherever our website is seen. I want so much to say to the children: Do you know who bought the Story Express for you? People from everywhere who have children, people from Georgia, Tennessee, Florida, Pennsylvania, Texas, Kansas, Kentucky, North Carolina, Alabama, Virginia, New York. (Have I named your state yet? You can correct that easily.)

Have we gotten enough money yet? No, but we will. We must be able to order the vehicle and prepare it soon so that the Story Express can start rolling this summer. We will publish pictures when it is ready.

Be sure to indicate on your check "For the Story Express." Our finances are like Captain Kangaroo's coat, with dozens of pockets. We want your check to go in the right pocket.

And my promise still stands: If gifts fall short, we will get the vehicle even if I have to set up a roadside stand and sell boiled peanuts.

(May)

NEVER BUY A VAN OFF THE RACK. If my mother said it once, she said it 100 times: "Never buy a van off the rack." Sure, you may save a few dollars shopping for one in a discount store that is loaded with hundreds of them, all the same style and color. But when, on the way home, you meet three dozen exactly like yours, you will be sick at your stomach.

And if you are buying one for the pleasure of children who never have anything new or special, you face a no-brainer: order one special and when it arrives, customize it.

That is exactly what we did. On April 29, we put in the order: white Sprinter Cargo van, not the small, not the medium, but the large, with the tall ceiling. If it carried passengers, it would seat 15, but it will not carry passengers. Transporting the children would be a major liability, not to mention insurance costs. We will transport singers and storytellers along with books, CDs, tapes, and musical instruments. The Story Express will pull in, be parked, the back doors opened wide, and children will come in, sit on the floor of the van, and enjoy. I can hardly wait.

When, then, will the van be delivered? I am not sure. A nationwide search is on for one already available, but the search may not be fruitful. But, no matter; the manufacturer will create what we want. And when will we get it? "This summer" is the only answer I can give you now.

And the price? About $36,500. And how much money do we have? In cash and pledges, $12,000. Then did we not order it prematurely? Oh, no. You do the math: $12,000 + friends like you = $36,500. See, I told you.

THERE WILL BE NO SLICK OKRA IN HEAVEN! That is the truth; otherwise, it would not be heaven but "the bad place." If that is not the truth, then I have suffered in vain.

And suffer I have. For reasons that still escape me, I was fed slick okra as a child. As punishment? I think not; I was obedient to my parents and said my prayers at night. As spiritual discipline? I think so, but such medieval practices must end.

For this reason, I will stand sentinel watch on Saturday evening, September 25, when all who desire will share dinner at Appalachian Weekend. It will be a bring-in, covered-dish meal. Do not worry; there will be plenty for guests and travelers from afar. In other words, don't bring lime Jell-O in the trunk of your car from Topeka. Those who do bring food will bring enough to share.

But do be warned: covered dishes will be uncovered, so do not try to smuggle in slick okra. Fried, yes, and black-eyed peas, collards, lima beans, corn on the cob, fried apples, cheese grits, squash, fruit salad, Brussels sprouts, green beans, even broccoli. None of these is contraband. But slick okra? You and your okra will be stopped at the door, and you will be cast into the outer darkness where there will be weeping and wailing and gnashing of teeth.

(June)

A CONSOLING WORD TO THOSE UPSET. It never occurred to me that the extraordinarily good news that the Story Express van is paid for would be upsetting to some. Yes, the van is paid for! Your gifts poured in, the money is in the bank, and upon delivery, a check will be written for the full amount. Paid in full. No balance due, no mortgage, no loan. Thank you, thank you, thank you. Calls are coming in: "I didn't think you could do it." "I knew you could do it." "God sure smiled on your program." "I'm proud to have been able to help."

And then this: "I didn't know you would get the money so fast; I was going to give something; I didn't think there was any hurry about it." The voice was sad. My heart went out.

Good news, my friend. When the van is delivered, it will be paid for, it's true. But there it will sit: without a license tag, without fuel, without insurance, and uncustomized. Unless—unless someone with thought and imagination says, "That van is not the Story Express without an Operation Fund."

I have asked Kay to set up an Operation Fund and then jump in her car and speed to the post office. You know how swiftly the gifts came before. And those who dilly-dallied and missed out: hurry, and maybe your gift will start the Story Express rolling.

I love it when good plans come together.

IS BLACKBERRY JAM ART? As you know, the display and sale of arts and crafts traditional in Appalachia will be an important part of Appalachian Weekend, September 25-26.

The question has arisen, would foods prepared in traditional fashion be regarded as an art or craft? Most certainly yes. For example, green beans sewn on a string and hung up to dry, ready for winter cooking, would be great. Such beans are called "leather britches." Or pumpkin, cut in rings and hung in the sun on a broom handle, would stir warm memories. And, of course, jams, jellies, preserves, pickles, sassafras roots, and cracklings. But please, no souse. Souse is neither art nor craft.

(July)

"THOU SHALT BARELY GET BY" is not the Eleventh Commandment. In fact, it is not a commandment at all; it is not even a guide for anyone's life. Even the poorest of the poor struggle to find in life a song, a poem, a touch of art, a sweet aroma, a kind of flourish that announces to the world, "I, too, am created in God's image." Years ago, a psychologist named Maslow classified needs in a person's life. He began with physical needs (food, clothing, etc.), followed by safety or security needs. Then came the need for love. At the top of his pyramid, and last of all, was the need for self-esteem, enrichment, and fulfillment. It makes a kind of sense.

However, at The Craddock Center we reverse the order. Of course, we try to address needs as they are presented to us; but in our programs for children we meet them with songs, art, dance, and story. In other words, we specialize in enrichment and self-esteem. We could justify what we do by quoting experts in child development, but we do not. We point to the children—laughing, listening, singing, and dancing. Ask them if they are poor and they will smile and say, "No."

And so, next month Head Start/Pre-K will begin again, and thanks to all of you who support The Craddock Center, 1,000 three- and four-year-olds will turn loose of Mother's skirt to which they cling with fear and tears, and begin to listen, to laugh, to sing, and to dance. In other words, they will meet our artists and their fun helpers.

Any questions? Then come visit, but come prepared for your heart to melt.

THE FOOD FIGHT STOPS HERE AND NOW. I have the right to stop it since I am the one who started it.

Yes, we are going to have the Saturday evening meal together during Appalachian Weekend, September 25-26. And yes, all who wish may eat with us. And yes, there will be plenty of food and it will be good and we will enjoy it.

But no, we will not serve all the stuff being volunteered. The announced "Bring a dish" plan is off, scuttled, dead, gone, and forgotten. I never dreamed when, in the last issue of *Milk & Honey,* I mentioned "souse" that I was opening the door to offers of chitterlings, pigs' feet, calf brains, groundhog, possum, turtle, and raccoon. I confess to having eaten some of these things, but the Depression is over. So save those dishes until your brother-in-law visits. For now, *we* will set the table—enjoy!

(August)

104 **DAYS AND COUNTING.** One hundred and four days ago, the plant where Dodge vans are made said, "Maybe sooner, but 120 days at the outside." For those not into industry-speak, "at the outside" means "no later than." For those who barely passed math, that means that in 16 days, Mountain Valley Motors will call saying, "A beautiful white van is here for The Craddock Center."

I will take the money you have given, receive the van, and drive it to the Center. Admirers will ooh and aah, and cameras will click. "Back away," I will admonish, "It isn't ready yet. We have to customize it and painters must decorate it. Then the van will be the Story Express."

"Will the Story Express be dedicated to God and to the children?" you ask. "Oh, yes, that will take place in the parking lot of the Kiwanis Building on Saturday, September 25, during Appalachian Weekend." All can admire it and be proud that they helped pay for it. Amazing, isn't it?

But a cynic, hardened by a lifetime of disappointments, asks, "You don't really believe that van will be delivered when they said, do you?"

"Yes, yes, I do. Believing and hoping is what I do. I have been doing it all my life. Feel free to join me."

2004

(October)

SAY CHEESE. Kay Zimbrick has given to the Center a very fine digital camera, and we are extremely grateful. Until now, we had to call on others to photograph our events.

But, you may ask, why did *we* not give *her* a camera as a going-away present instead of the one going away giving one to us? Let me explain. While she was working here as administrator, Kay was permitted to run errands and handle chores for which she was not paid. She was left free to work extra hours without imbursement. She was allowed to pay for small expenditures out of her own purse without reimbursement. Kay even enjoyed the promise of pay raises that never, in fact, materialized. Now that she is going, why should we do a 180 and start being nice to her? So, I ask you, who should give whom a camera? I rest my case.

Some have asked for Kay's phone number in order to thank her for her extraordinary work for the Center. If you do call her, it is best to call before 8:00 a.m. our time, which is 5:00 a.m. her time. After that, she is unavailable, lolling at the beach, in a Jacuzzi, or in a hammock. Please respect her valuable time.

Thank you, Kay, for everything.

(November)

IT HURTS, BUT I UNDERSTAND when someone turns down our request for financial support with the response, "We give to the poor but to programs that meet their *real* needs." Meaning, of course, food and clothing, especially at Christmas.

Blessings on those programs; who could deny food and clothing to a child? The Craddock Center has a small emergency fund and not a week goes by without at least one claim on that purse. But that is not our primary mission. We are about the business of enriching lives, of lifting self-esteem, of instilling a sense of self-worth, of effecting socialization so that each child can play and study and grow as an equal to other children. We do

9

this through songs, art, and stories. Studies show that participating in such programs increases a child's success in school and in life in the community.

The records of some charities indicate that they give to children just as they gave to their parents and to their grandparents. Generation after generation the story continues the same.

Our goal is to break the cycle, to change the story. There are 13 million children living in depressing poverty in this country. But we get up each morning believing our small effort is making and will continue to make a difference. And every dollar we receive is an investment in that difference, and, on behalf of the children, we thank you.

(December)

OK, OK, SO WE ARE RUNNING LATE. What are you going to do, shoot me? As I reflect on all the noises I made last spring and summer about how we would get the van from the factory in Germany, have it properly decorated on the outside and customized on the inside, dedicated and on the road by the beginning of the school year 2004-05, I am almost embarrassed.

But not quite—you see, the sight of it simply melts the delays away and we all say, "Who cares? Just look at it!" Have you looked at the Story Express on our website (www.craddockcenter.org)? I would tell you to come by the Center and see it, but it is sometimes here, sometimes not. Sometimes Ron Zimbrick and Larry Hansen have to take it on location to do the customizing for sight, sound, recording, computerizing, etc. (I use *etc.* when I don't know what I am talking about.)

We are ready. Sit by your front window; it will pass your house soon, and you don't want to miss it.

2005

(January)

AND TWO VIOLINS. Perhaps you, as I am, are commemorating the 200th anniversary of the Lewis and Clark Expedition to the great Northwest part of this country. On flatboats, in canoes, and on foot, 32 men spent three painful years traversing inhospitable terrain, often among suspicious if not hostile natives, keeping journals and marking trails. Inclement weather, disease, hunger, feet torn by thorns, and boats dashed on rocks slowed but did not stop them. They had to anticipate needs, pack accordingly, and leave behind what was not essential.

In the baggage of what was essential for the journey were two violins. Strange? Not at all. Music is as necessary for human life as are dry socks and coffee beans. At least that is what we believe here at the Center. And so we sing and tell stories and enjoy awakening the human spirit in small children.

Come visit and see for yourself.

(February)

DO YOU HAVE ANY IDEA what it is like to walk around with 37 pounds of untold stories inside you? Well, that is my miserable condition since we had to cancel Songs and Stories at Brasstown. I'm not the only one miserable; over 400 folk were primed and ready. Some even braved the weather and went to Brasstown, but it was no night to be out. Sure, we could have sung and talked to 50 people, but when you are big stars of radio, stage, and screen, empty chairs are depressing. It pulls the air right out of you, and when you pull the air out of my stories, there's precious little left.

My doctor has suggested that when the burden of these untold stories becomes too great, just unload one or two on unsuspecting strangers. They may or may not enjoy the stories, but you sure will feel better. Sounds like good advice. I think I will try it now. Have you ever been to Big Stone Gap, Virginia? There's a woman there, in her eighties now, who never remarried after shooting her husband. Killed him, and confessed it to the court, but the jury . . .

This is not working, is it? The bad weather on January 29 just ruined everything.

(March)

HERE'S THE DEAL. At the Center we believe in books, books that parents and teachers read to children, books children read, books young people read, books adults read. And we give away lots of books to children, hoping to begin a lifetime of reading. Books are given at Head Start, and the Story Express has been customized with bookshelves in order to deliver books.

"How much does it cost to fill the Story Express with books?" I was asked recently. "About $2,000," I said.

"Well, here's the deal," said this friend of our program, "I'll give you $6,000 to fill it three times, but you have to match it with $6,000 from another person or from other persons."

"It's a deal," I said, and we shook hands. Now I have to get a gift of $6,000 for books. Any ideas? I sure hate to have to hit the streets with a tin cup. I'm not too proud to do it, mind you. These kids are important to me. But I'm getting on in years, my legs are going, and I hate to look pitiful. People give to the pitiful, but the program of the Center is not a pitiful program. We don't want to give that impression, do we?

How about this: if you gave us $6,000, I would immediately call the deal maker, we would have $12,000 in the book fund, we would be able to fill the Story Express six times, and children all over Southern Appalachia would be hearing and reading those books that thrilled you years ago.

I'm really liking this idea. I will be checking P.O. Box 69 at the Cherry Log Post Office. No, not tomorrow; you need time to get to *your* post office.

THE HELEN LEWIS LECTURE WAS A SUCCESS, if you measure success by the warm reception given to Sonny Houston and the Blue Velvet Band. Their opening set put us emotionally and appreciatively in Appalachia.

You measure success by the size of the crowd. Such a large response to the first annual lecture bodes well for this event in subsequent years.

You measure success by the lingering of the crowd to continue savoring the program and to exchange stories. "Please, go home, we have to lock the building."

You measure success by applause twice given to our guest lecturer, Loyal Jones of Berea, Kentucky. His vast knowledge of Appalachia, gained by research and personal experience, was delightfully wrapped in the humor and stories of the region. The laughter of the crowd was sprinkled with a few "Amens," or from old-timers: "That is the way it is."

You measure success by the multiple ovations given to Helen Lewis whom we honor with this lectureship. She is a national treasure.

You measure success by the gratitude we feel toward the Blue Ridge Mountain Arts Association, our host for the evening. The old courtroom was prepared for us, and for the entire evening the jury was sequestered and the judge delayed. It was our party.

A Taste of Milk & Honey

(April)

IT HAS COME TO MY ATTENTION or, more correctly, it has been brought to my attention; otherwise, it would not have come to my attention at all. And I speak to you about the matter not as an admission of oversight or attempt to mislead. On the contrary, I declare here and now my innocence and resist every call to repentance. Of course, I am capable of error, and were the occasion ever to arise in which I was at fault, I am confident that rather than resorting to pulverizing logic to defend myself, I would squeeze out a tear capable of washing away the flaw. But is this such an occasion? No siree, Bob. I name no names, but you know these detractors, these who lie in wait, who slither among the jots and tittles, who major in minors, who exaggerate, who proclaim apocalyptic importance in every trifling charge that someone has painted outside the lines.

Now that I have calmed myself, I proceed directly to the charge. To wit: that in the March issue of *Milk & Honey* I did brazenly request that someone give to the Center $6,000 to match the $6,000 gift for children's books already offered. Now it is true that the $6,000 for books is a matching gift. And it is also true that I took a few sentences to relish the thought that in one gift the match would be made and these hills would resound with joy. As Shakespeare would say, "'Tis a consummation devoutly to be wished." Forgive me if I tarried too long over that pleasant prospect.

But did I thereby exclude from the book project the participation of those unable to contribute the total sum? By no means! No, a thousand times, no! Have I been so long with you and you do not know me? The very thought is paralyzing; I think I will take to my bed.

I have been comforted by the number of gifts coming in, not only proving that many of you heard me all right, but also confirming the philosophy of the Center: no gift is so small as to be unimportant. The more people who feel ownership in our program, no matter how small their purses, the more we are affirmed in the rightness and importance of what we do.

The mail has just arrived, and I am even more comforted. Without doubt, within the month I will be totally comforted. Your generosity will have covered as with a blanket the confusion created, or so it is charged, by misspeaking, the children will have their books, and the hills will be alive with the sound of music.

It will be my good fortune to announce in the May issue of *Milk & Honey* that the total of your gifts has exceeded the $6,000 sought. All doubters are free to stay, but you must stand and join in singing the doxology.

MY FEELINGS WEREN'T HURT when we received recently a check for $100 to be used to improve the appearance of the entrance to The Craddock Center. In other words, get two shrubs and some flowers. We will do just that, and we are grateful. In my opinion the check was not a commentary on how drab our entrance is but rather a compliment saying, "For only $100 your place would look nice." Thanks.

Or maybe it was a compliment on how attractive our entrance is. After all, a mother does not put a ribbon in her little girl's hair to make her pretty but because she already is. Thanks.

Or maybe the check was a compliment to our use of money received. When we receive a gift for our programs, it is used 100% for our programs. In fact, we are delightfully embarrassed by our low-budget maintenance. Toward the children we are generous, toward ourselves we are penny-pinchers.

So, maybe the check said, "We know you won't dip into program money to brighten your front door, so here, use this."

I like that. Thanks.

(May)

O, FOR A THOUSAND TONGUES and then I could express the gratitude of 1,000 children who say to you, "thank you." It is important, whether you gave little or much, that you know you have blessed children you probably will never meet. I want you to know that last August most of these children came into Head Start classrooms afraid, silent, or crying, hiding behind Mother. This month they ran out of those rooms laughing and singing. Thanks to you, they have songs to sing all summer, stories to tell all summer, and books to take to their parents with a new request: "Read me a story."

Not all the beautiful changes in the children are due to our program; of course not. Most, but not all, come from homes that are poor in things but rich in love. The Head Start schools have good teachers who care for the children. But the Head Start programs are strapped for funds and word out of Washington brings the tragic news of further cuts. Budgets are trim, with no funds for programs of enrichment—music, art, storytelling, and dance. And so, through The Craddock Center, you come into their classrooms singing, dancing, telling stories. You have enriched their lives, and if the statistics are to be believed, you have improved their chances for success in school and in life. So, thank you. I hope you will join us in August to begin a new year.

It has been my pleasure to visit some of the schools. To be sure, with some children there is evidence of physical and emotional abuse and it breaks your heart. But the overwhelming experience is one of delight. You look at each new face and say, "This is a child of God. I see a striking resemblance."

(August)

I'VE BEEN HAVING TROUBLE retiring. I am now in my third retirement, and it is not working out. With all this work, when did I have time to work when I was working? And I am just a volunteer, for goodness sake! I don't get it.

I talked with a friend of mine who is an expert on retirement. He retired the day he finished his schooling. How he has managed to be on the payroll of various churches I don't know. He is now retired from those long years of retirement. It seemed natural to seek his counsel about my problem.

"Don't retire all at once," he said. "Ease into it."

"And how do I do that?"

"Just don't show up. If you show up, people will think you are willing to work, and before you know it, there are phone calls, appointments, trips, speeches, etc. Just don't show up."

I am going to try it. Starting in September, every Friday I am not going to show up. I'm serious; I will not be here. Ask Tammy, and she will tell you I didn't show up.

(September)

WHAT RIGHT HAVE YOU TO BE MERRY? This is the question Ebenezer Scrooge asked his nephew when the nephew greeted his uncle with a "Merry Christmas!" Scrooge knew the nephew to be living in cold and gnawing poverty, and with a crippled child. Good question: What right have you to be merry?

This is the question my family asked itself when a wedding fell within a week of a funeral. This is the question I asked of my dirt-poor parishioners in Appalachia when they continued to plant flowers in ground that would grow potatoes. This is the question asked of the little girl dancing to radio music outside her cardboard hovel in South Africa. This is the question asked of the USO, sponsoring dances for soldiers in wartime. This is the question asked of the children chasing balloons in the rubble of their Biloxi home. This is the question we ask ourselves as we host Cherokee Indians to help us celebrate Appalachian Weekend in the very county where the Trail of Tears had one of its most cruel beginnings.

What right, indeed? None, I guess; none at all. That is, if the right to be merry is given only to those who prosper, who have kept hunger and violence and injustice and death from their door. But still in ourselves and in unlikely others, there can be found profound joy and tenacious hope.

17

That is, if joy comes not from the circumstance but from trust in the final goodness of a God who prepares a table in the presence of enemies and who walks beside us through the valley of the shadow of death.

(November)

THE REPORT OF MY DEATH IS JUST A RUMOR. In fact, there have been two such rumors in recent weeks. One person who heard it did have the decency to call to see if it were true. But please, don't call the office; it is upsetting to Tammy. You see, some mornings I walk in the office feeling and looking borderline and it creates a climate of uncertainty, which is not a good working environment. In addition, there is not much job security working for someone who has passed away.

So, leave Tammy out of it. If you want to know, call me at home. If Nettie answers, ask for me, and if I come to the phone, that is a clue. If I don't come to the phone, then ask Nettie. She probably will know; she keeps up with where I am, pretty much.

2006

NO CHARGE. Some of the friends of the Center have advised that funds for our programs, always in need of funds, could be raised by charging admission to events we offer the public. It is thoughtful and reasonable advice, and you can be sure it has laid a claim on my mind more than once. When persons with large incomes, large homes, and long vacations show up, I say to myself, "They are able to pay, they are accustomed to paying, they probably expect to pay, so why no charge?" In fact, I continue the conversation with myself, "Some of these more prosperous friends may be embarrassed to enter without paying. Why embarrass them? Take their money."

Let me address first the obvious. There is no desire to embarrass anyone, neither those who can pay nor those who cannot. I am also aware that in our culture that which is offered free is by many assumed to be of inferior quality. If it is free it must not be worth charging for. Nothing could be further from the truth. The lectures, the music, the seminars we offer the community are first rate. And the music, the stories, the books we give to Head Start children are the best available. No worn-out, second-hand, hand-me-down gifts that would only say to the children, "You are not worth the best."

Having said that, let me remind you, the vision of the Center is the eventual creation of a community that is one community. We are not naïve: there are haves and have-nots, advantaged and disadvantaged, and the differences show in our residences, lifestyles, and, regrettably, also in our churches. But is it not great now and then to gather for music or seminar

19

or lecture where those differences are not honored? No one enters by the "pay" gate and no one enters by the "poor" gate; all enter the "free" gate. And when we sit together, we have a brief but very important experience of the kingdom of God. I hope it is not irreverent to say that this arrangement reminds one of grace. Grace comes to all without distinction.

Of course, some send gifts that pay the bills for all of us, and we are endlessly grateful. But if for a day or for an evening, those who give and those who receive share an event for which there is no charge, perhaps someone with courage and imagination will think of other and more lasting ways to remove distinctions among us. Would you like that?

In the meantime, *Come on in and make yourself at home: there is no charge.*

"HE IS SLOW," SHE SAID. I knew what she meant; she is his teacher and knows that he lags behind his peers in the classroom and on the playground. It was evident to me, a visitor for the day. But it seemed not to be evident to him; he seemed happy to appropriate life at the pace given him. Whether he will gradually move to the pace of others as he matures, of course, I do not know.

I do know that I am also slow. Not the slowness that comes with age, although that, too. But I have always been slow. This is not a commentary on my physical condition; I have had the ability to run and jump with the best of them, but why should I? A slower pace allows me to think, to reflect, to muse, to assimilate, and to process. That I am slow is not a commentary on school performance. I found the demands of school rather easy to negotiate, allowing me time to slow down, time to savor the wisdom and skill of those who came to me in books. Why rush to finish homework in an hour when you could spend an entire evening with Shakespeare, or Milton, or Poe, or Melville, or DuBois, or Plato?

And every day I am more aware how slow I am. Everyone else is multitasking, taking advantage of the speed and immediate availability of all people and all knowledge. Even the music is fast; my ear is able to catch only a word now and then. Mind you, I am not setting you up for an argument against speed or in favor of my pace. I am comfortable in the pace given me.

However, a close friend did raise with me the question: Have you ever wondered what you could have achieved if you had quickened your pace a bit?

No. Probably even less.

(February)

THE ARITHMETIC OF FAITH: $140, the cost of providing a Head Start child our Children's Enrichment Program. The number she gives me is a fact, a flat-out actual total, double-checked, triple-tallied, scout's honor, hand on the Bible, just ask the auditor, no ifs, ands, or buts, take it to the bank, true sum. That is her job: good, bad, or indifferent, give me the truth. She is not paid to ease the pain or subdue a doxology; I can handle the truth. I need no hymns softly sung, no explanations about the economy, no speculations about errors in the post office, no covering for those who always mean well.

So I give her the level gaze and ask without emotion: Is this the true total?

Without a flinch, she answers: Yes.

At that moment, spontaneously and simultaneously, we burst into song. The doxology is the only proper response. You have remembered the children and given generously. Given our rather small mailing list, the percentage of responses is extraordinary. The children thank you and we thank you.

Then I take Tammy's report, go into my office and close the door. You see, in her office all the machines calculate and report only the facts. She has no machine that registers hope, or perhaps, or maybe.

But I do. So I sit down and do the arithmetic of faith:

228	Scholarships received. Thank you.
11	Scholarships to be sent once I locate that pledge card.
9	"Can I send a check without the card?" Of course.
8	Scholarships to be sent once we return from vacation.
9	Scholarships, "I told you I will and I will."
10	Scholarships, "I sent one but my wife says we should send two." (Your wife is a saint.)
7	Scholarships, "Here's the money for half; maybe someone else can afford only half."
282	**Total**

This is absolutely amazing! I almost said unbelievable, but that would not be true: it *is* believable.

(March)

WHAT WILL FRED DO NOW? If you read the article about Teri Slemons coming to work at the Center, then this is a natural question. Let me answer as best I can.

First, Teri is not coming to do what I have been doing; she is coming to do what I have *not* been doing. That's why she is coming; it has not been getting done. What do you think I am—qualified? Have I been so long with you and you haven't seen the glaring need for Teri?

Secondly, I have options. I could retire again. The sleep sounds good. I sleep well at night, fairly well in the morning, but in the afternoon, I just toss and turn. Or, I could open a roadside stand and sell fishing bait, do a little motorcycle repair, and practice acupuncture. Or, I could do a better job of what I do.

Finally, what I will do is conduct Preaching Workshops, tell stories, educate the public about our programs, make more friends for the Center, and raise funds, both operational and permanent.

We must raise more financial support in order to grow our programs to meet more needs. I will keep trying to do that, accepting any success as pure grace. I may drop by to see you. What's for supper?

(April)

WHY DIDN'T I THINK OF IT BEFORE? In the last issue of *Milk & Honey*, we were at 255 scholarships ($140 for each child) for our Children's Enrichment Program. The goal was 282. Motivating friends of children to reach the goal and finish the campaign was the challenge, what to do? Tears, begging, threats, sermonettes, favorite Scripture citations; my bag of tricks was empty.

In desperation I fell back on my 40 years in the classroom: I set a deadline. All inclined to give scholarships had until April 15 to do so.

The response has been amazing. We had 255, the goal was 282, we now have 294! Of course, notes accompanied many checks: "I'm ahead of the deadline; do I get extra credit?" "I delayed my funeral in order to get this in the mail." "I hope this arrives on time; I'm in a dog sled race across Alaska." And, of course, the usual requests for extensions: "My aunt died again." "I gave my check to the mailman, but he has come down with leprosy."

I enjoyed all the notes; it seemed like old times. A deadline still works its irritating magic.

But it's not the deadline, it's you and your generosity and your love for the children. Thanks.

YOU CAN DO THIS, AND WE CAN HELP. Spend the night, that is, during Appalachian Weekend, September 29-30. You see, this year the schedule is different. On Friday night the Welsh Men's Choir will sing, along with some local singing groups. Miss that and you'll kick yourself all the way back to Idaho. And then Saturday morning and afternoon, singers and musicians from all over Appalachia will perform. Miss that and you'll eat rat poison and die.

Already I know of persons coming from Texas, Illinois, and Florida, plus gobs of folk coming up from Atlanta.

THERE IS SOME MISUNDERSTANDING about my relation to the Center now that Teri Slemons is directing the day-to-day operation.

Here's the deal. I remain as Director of Development and as consultant to Teri. There will be no change in the purpose and vision of the Center; I simply will focus on making more friends and supporters for the Center.

But do I still have an office at the Center? You bet your bottom dollar I do. In fact, I have an even bigger office. I was officed in the front bedroom (our place was a three-bedroom home), but now I am in the large eating area off the kitchen. I have a telephone, wastebasket, and everything. This bigger room allows me to use all my office furniture: three lazy boys and a couch. Come see me.

(May)

OUR SQUARE TABLE IS ACTUALLY ROUND when preachers come to the Center to discuss preaching. They do, you know, in groups of 4 to 12, from far and near, from large churches and small, with and without years of experience. All we ask is when, how many, and how long. Oh yes, we do ask that the group make an offering to the Center. Lunch is served at the Center so we can also eat together.

And the table is round: no pecking order, no preferential treatment, no question out of order or unimportant. I could talk all day about preaching, but I try not to. The questions brought by participants are primary.

When we reach the end of our time together, we are never finished; we just quit. Look at this sampling of questions that have arisen, and you'll see why we never finish.

- Did you ever preach what you yourself did not believe?
- What is meant by Scripture being inspired?
- Are all preachers hypocrites, not living up to their own words?

24

- Are churches more suspicious of preachers or am I paranoid?
- After I preach, I can't remember what I said. Is that normal?
- My family doesn't attend services anymore. Should I resign?
- Why do I feel more comfortable preaching outside the pulpit?
- Would getting feedback on my sermons be beneficial?
- I don't think I should preach on every issue that arises. Am I a coward?
- Tell me again exactly what pulpit plagiarism is.
- Will I ever lose my stage fright?
- My associate is a better preacher than I am. Now what?
- Where can I get help in choosing commentaries?
- I want compliments but do not handle them well. Why?
- Should I preach when I feel I have nothing to say?
- Will visual media replace preaching?
- Walk us through your preparation process, and go slow.

(June)

BOY, WAS I FOOLED. The clerk said it was a hammock; I paid for a hammock; it looked like a hammock; it fit the hammock space in my new "office" (the Greek word is "kitchen"); when I lay down on it, my body confirmed that it was a hammock.

Boy, was I fooled! I had hardly relaxed when the thing took off like a magic carpet. A tag on the underside flapped in the wind: it read "Magic Carpet for the Unable to Retire."

Zoom! I was at the Birmingham UMC on the north side of Atlanta. Yes, Birmingham is in Georgia now. Strong winds lately. Sorry, Alabama. A great church, strong pastoral leadership, warm welcome to the pulpit, and generous to The Craddock Center.

Zoom! Hello, Charlotte, North Carolina. Preaching Workshop for about 40 moving-toward-ordination preachers. Wedding for Jolin Wilks, the artist who sketched the faces of our Head Start children last year. Preached in her stead at First Christian while she left on her honeymoon. (There are other ways to avoid preaching besides getting married, for goodness sake!)

Zoom! Amarillo, Texas. Same as I remembered: warm, windy, open, friendly, honest, and welcoming to me. A large group gathered for a presentation of The Craddock Center programs and then a sermon. Generous to the Center with the promise of more.

Zoom! Never been to Avon Lakes, Ohio (suburb of Cleveland) before, but felt quite at home. Have known the pastor of the United Church of Christ for years. She offered me the pulpit and on Monday hosted 50 preachers for a workshop.

Zoom! Back to Cherry Log where I will for three Sundays teach Sunday School at Cherry Log Christian Church. And then—

Zoom! By the time you read this I will have been to Washington, D.C. where an attorney friend is hosting a light dinner for 12 to 14 potential donors to The Craddock Center. After my presentation, I will fly home. This is my first such event. Sounds promising. Interested in being a host?

If no takers, I will return the magic carpet and sue the furniture store for $9 million. We can use the money.

(July)

I HATE BEING PRESSURED, but after a while a poor fellow caves in to it. At least that is what I am doing.

For the last month I have been constantly interrogated, the same two questions over and over again. One, how did that Fund Raiser in Washington go? Two, is that plan portable to other places?

The answer to the first question is "It went very well." I asked Chrys Lemon, an attorney friend, to host a light dinner, inviting a few of his friends who might be interested in the program of The Craddock Center. After dinner, I would make a brief presentation, answer questions, and invite gifts to the Center. He did; there were 13 present. I did; there was clear interest. And they did; they gave $12,570 and one promise. How did it go? It went quite well.

The answer to the second question is, "Yes, the plan is portable." Let me know, we will choose a date, you invite friends who might be interested to a breakfast, lunch, or light dinner, give me 30 minutes for a presentation, and you are done. How much donation would be a success? Anything above my travel expenses would be welcome. But as they say, "The more the merrier."

You have my number; I'll wait for your call. Many dates are available, but don't ask for June 9. That is our wedding anniversary and I have to take Nettie to the Pink Pig for barbeque. I'm sure you're aware of the pressure I am under.

(August)

THE GIFT. On December 30, 2004, a memorial service was held at Cherry Log Christian Church for Joe Burke. On August 3, 2006, an impressive gift to The Craddock Center was made by Joe Burke. You probably want a word of clarification.

Joe kept on a nightstand near his bed, along with his glasses, an oval metal box into which he put loose change from his pockets. Now and then a small withdrawal was made in response to a claim too small for a check or paper money, but, in general, the coins accumulated.

Joe died, and suddenly every reminder of him became sacred and irremovable. Doris did not move his glasses. We hang on to what we can. Doris did not touch the box of coins. She certainly could not bring herself to spend any of it; the idea of it seemed sacrilegious. For 19 months the box and the glasses stayed in place.

Then Doris read Teri's article in the July issue of *Milk & Honey* about Coins for The Craddock Center. She knew Joe would have wanted the box of coins given to the Center, and so, on August 3, 2006, Doris came to the Center and gave the box of coins to Tammy, along with a note to me explaining what I have now told you.

Tammy took the coins to the bank to have them sorted and counted by that thingamajig that does it in the blink of an eye: $43.76 total, said the machine. I wanted a second opinion. I held the box of coins before the wide eyes of one of the Center children. "Wow! There must be a million dollars in there!" She was exactly right.

Thanks, Joe. Thanks, Doris.

(October)

ONLY THE PLACE HAS BEEN CHANGED.
The Program: "Winged for the Heart," Songs and Stories by Dr. Steve Darsey and Dr. Fred Craddock. (No change)
The Date: The last Saturday of January. In 2007, that is January 27. (No change)
The Time: 8:00 p.m. (No change)
The Audience: All who wish to join us. No charge, but an offering is taken. (No change)
The Place: The Performing Arts Center at Fannin County High School in Blue Ridge, Georgia. We were scheduled out of our usual time at Brasstown; but this room is larger, more comfortable, better acoustics, better lighting. Steve likes it, I like it, and you will like it. Tammy will provide directions for out-of-towners. Why not rent a cabin with a fireplace and make a weekend of it? More later.

I'm getting excited.

RESILIENCE. In a recent seminar for ministers in Kansas City, I was teamed with psychiatrist and long-time friend, Dr. Betty Bashaw. In our discussions of displacement, disappointment, and violence, Dr. Bashaw introduced the subject of resilience. She pointed out that persons who have experienced poverty, family breakups, and even death in the family, if resilient, can adapt and live successful, fruitful lives.

And what makes for resilience? Among several factors, two especially impressed me: 1) the encouragement and emotional connection with an adult outside the family, and 2) the ability to read early and experience a love of books. (Dr. Bashaw cited a study by Werner and Smith.)

I thought of our Children's Enrichment Program and was quietly proud. Well, not too quietly: I mentioned it to a few dozen.

But I especially wanted you to know.

FINALLY, A SPEAKING FEE after over 50 years of being without one. I know it has been frustrating for those inviting me to their churches or related groups. It would have been simpler for them and me: a yes or no would follow, without discussion.

But not having a required fee was my feeble attempt to be available to small churches as well as large, those with money and those without. So my hosts determined honorarium, and, on balance, usually gave me more than I deserved.

Now, however, I have a set fee. My fee is this: make a gift to the Center. What size gift? All you can possibly afford. Take it or leave it. I will not budge a penny. I have no Plan B; this is it. I will not negotiate.

(November)

THE EIGHT MOST FREQUENTLY ASKED QUESTIONS IN THE WORLD.

1. Will Fred Craddock and Steve Darsey have the Songs and Stories program this year? Yes.
2. When will it be? Saturday, January 27, 2007, at 8:00 p.m.
3. Will it be at the same place? No. Brasstown Valley Resort gave our date to another event, so we have moved to the Performing

Arts Center in Blue Ridge, Georgia. The room is larger with better acoustics, lighting, and view of the stage.

4. How can I get a ticket? The event is free. We used tickets in the past to keep the audience at 400, the limit of the room. Our new location will seat twice this number, so there is no need for tickets. There will be a free-will offering to cover rent of the room, sound engineer, janitorial services, etc.

5. Are there good places to eat and to spend the night? Yes, restaurants and lodgings a-plenty.

6. How do I find this Performing Arts Center? From Appalachian Highway 515, aka US 76, head east on old Highway 76 (the intersection where you see June Walker Chevrolet). Follow the road until you see the Performing Arts Center at Fannin County High School on a large hill on your right.

7. Will CDs of previous performances be available for purchase? Yes.

8. Will I have a good time? Is the Pope Catholic?

(December)

EVEN THE POOR HAVE A RIGHT TO THEIR PRETTIES, so Mrs. Glover reminded me years ago. I was a young minister in Roane County, Tennessee, and had appointed myself economic advisor to the poor among whom I worked. To the families at or below poverty level, I sternly cautioned: potatoes and beans and fatback, not flowers and candles and candy. They turned a deaf ear to my wise counsel. I repeated myself, with volume increased. Nothing. Nothing, that is, except the protesting voice of old Mrs. Glover: "Even the poor have a right to their pretties."

She was right, of course. My memory told me she was right. In the poverty of my rural childhood, my sister, my brothers, and I were treated to fanciful and full-winged stories by our father, and our mother joined us in stringing popcorn and wild berries, making chains of colored paper, and cutting out paper bells. A welcomed snow meant lots of snow cream, and sorghum became, in one afternoon, delicious taffy. Add gingerbread and milk and it was Christmas. "I wonder how the poor are doing," said our father.

The church speaks often and appropriately of good and evil, of right and wrong, of true and false. But the church could, and no less appropriately, speak often, and certainly at Christmas, of the beautiful and the ugly. If the church has trouble finding a Scripture text to justify it, then quote Mrs. Glover. She knows.

2007

(January)

I DON'T KNOW HOW OLD I REALLY AM. Let me explain. We had a calendar in my childhood home. The Depression was on and luxuries did not exist, but we had a calendar. It was a large calendar, hanging in the kitchen on the wall beside the fireplace. We seldom used that fireplace since the cookstove heated the kitchen. The calendar came from a drugstore, and it carried bold advertisements of Lydia Pinkham's Compound. At suppertime, on the last day of each month, with some ceremony and wise sayings about the passing of time, Momma tore off that month, revealing a new month about which she spoke with hope for better days. After supper Daddy cut the numbers of the old month into squares and taught us games with the numbers. He called it "ciphering."

One year, at the end of November, Momma inadvertently tore off both November and December. She laid December on a table, while on the wall Lydia Pinkham was boldly announcing January. The putting of January of the next year at the end of every calendar was well intended, I am sure, but in our home that year it proved to be disconcerting and confusing. We still had December, to be sure, but it was on the table, and from the table Daddy took it. Meaning no harm, with no malice aforethought, and totally unaware of the anxieties about to be released, he rolled December into a taper, stuck one end into the fire, lit his roll-your-own cigarette, and tossed the still burning taper on the hearth where it burned itself out. December was gone.

32

We had good parents and they did the best they could guessing what day it was. But guessing won't cut it in December; December has Christmas in it. No child should have to ask: "Is it Christmas yet?" And certainly no child should get the answer: "We're not sure." But awful as all this was, an even darker thought hung heavy in the mind: How many other months have been lost in similar fashion? Have there been other 11-month years? Or perhaps 10-month years?

So all my life, I have made adjustments in my calculations, and, I must admit, usually in my favor. Am I 43 years old? I'll take that. But on honest days (and they are few) when someone asks, "Fred, how old are you?" I come clean and say, "Probably 107, give or take."

In the meantime, Happy New Year, whenever that is.

(February)

WHY ME AND NOT STEVE? We had a great time at the Songs and Stories program on Saturday evening, January 27. At least I did, and Steve said he did, and many of you said you did.

But soon came the questions: Did a woman in whose home you were a guest really put cornflakes in your bed? Were you really served a meal of nothing but corn on the cob? Did you really know a man who could blow smoke rings through a hole in his side? Can you really tell if a watermelon is ripe by placing a broom straw across it? On and on the questions come; there seems to be no end to it.

And they were all addressed to me. Why not quiz Steve? He sang about a conversation between a possum and a raccoon. Did anyone ask Steve if it really happened? Did anyone ask Steve if a mule really put its hind feet in its mouth and kicked itself to death? Did anyone ask Steve if he really went up Cripple Creek to see his girl? Did anyone question Steve about Biling Cabbage Down? No; I asked Steve if there were any questions about his songs and he said, "Not a single one."

"And you, Fred, did anyone question whether your stories really happened?" A regular barrage of questions it was.

Oh, my friends, there is much doubt in our world. Unbelief is everywhere. It is painful to try to make your witness in the face of disbelief. I'm already questioning whether next year I should tell about riding a pig in a Fourth of July parade. Somebody might even doubt that. What's a fellow to do?

I know this; from now on I'll bring my Bible and place my hand on it before I ever open my mouth. That will surely silence the doubters and restore good old-fashioned faith that believes everything. Amen? Amen.

(March)

HAVE YOU NOTICED how many good people there are? I mean really good people? I don't have a better word to describe them: they are fundamentally good. Theirs is character you can trust. They do not take what is not theirs; they share what is. When they say Yes, they mean Yes, and you don't have to keep reminding them that they said Yes. They will postpone or even abandon their own plans because your need is urgent. They are generous, whether they have much or little. They tell the truth, but are not judgmental. They are not intrusive, but they are at your door when you thought no one knew you were at the end of your rope. You can depend on them. They never intend to harm. They do not need an audience before doing what is right. They mind their own business, which includes standing up for the unjustly treated. They are compassionate, but they do not use your misfortunes to display their compassion. They don't even know how to be cruel.

To be sure, not all have the most becoming personalities and, if left to you, a few changes would be made: take the cap off in the house; use a fork instead of a spoon; don't talk so loud; lose the profanity; clean up the jokes; help a bit more with the kids and the grandkids; don't go to work so early the rest of us feel guilty; vote for the right candidates for a change.

But in the long run, I can tolerate the bad habit or the prickly personality because these are good people; I mean really good people.

I add to my list of good people every day.

You're on it, by the way.

(April)

A FUNNY THING HAPPENED ON THE WAY TO THE PULPIT of University Church of Loma Linda University in southern California. The University as well as the Church is part of that fellowship of believers called Seventh Day Adventists. The welcome, the hospitality, the evidences of God's grace, the worship, all that one associates with a healthy church, were there in abundance. I was invited to preach and I happily accepted. The occasion was their usual Sabbath service.

On the way to the pulpit, I was asked to stop briefly in a small room off the chancel. There a woman introduced herself and explained that she prepared the preachers for television. The service was to be televised, as was their custom, and she was the makeup artist. I was suddenly not at home. I tried to be light: "Will this involve surgery? How could you possibly improve on this? Please, don't cause them to think Robert Redford is preaching today!"

She dulled the shine on my head, hid a blotch or two, and said, "Go get 'em, George!"

I said, "George? My name is Fred."

She said, "Sorry, I was thinking George Clooney." She was gracious and pleasant, but the light banter hardly concealed my being ill at ease.

Why was I ill at ease? Once I was in the pulpit, I was completely unaware of cosmetic or camera. All that was gone as I was now present to the worshipers and to the Gospel. But I have thought of it several times since; in fact, I am talking to you about it because it is again on my mind.

Do you have any idea why I was ill at ease in the makeup room? What do you think?

(May)

No, I AM NOT WRITING FROM JAIL thanks to Teri Slemons. You see, I thought that securing from the IRS our status of a 501(c)3 organization (tax exempt) was the alpha and omega of our legal duties. Teri came on board, asked me a string of questions about registrations, permits, forms, and documents, managed a thin smile in response to my shrug of the shoulders, offered a prayer in my behalf ("Father, forgive him, he knows not what he is doing"), and went to work.

Exactly 3,427,984 forms later, Teri lifted her weary face from her laptop and announced, "We are now legal." Always one for a party, I went straight for the Center's small pantry. "Thank God that's over!"

"Not quite," said Teri, "in seven months it will be 2008."

I hear every day about undocumented workers. Sounds great; where do we sign up?

(June)

How FAR CAN YOU REMEMBER? I know the question is strange. It is possible I misunderstood what was said; the question was not put to me. I overheard it at the Cherry Log Community Center at one of the regular Thursday evening at 6:00 gatherings of pickers, fiddlers, and assorted other musicians (come on down!). During a break in the music I moved into a small group already in conversation. The topic was fading memory in old age.

There were sad stories of Alzheimer's, funny stories of parking lot confusion, misplaced keys, and going to church the wrong day. Then one in the group asked another, "How far can you remember?" There was no immediate reply; perhaps because the question was strange. At least it was to me; I had never before heard anyone associate memory and distance. How far can you remember?

The one who asked began to answer his own questions. "When I was younger, I could remember as far as China, but now I can barely remember as far as Little Rock." I was puzzled. "Have you ever been to China?" "Lord no; I've never even been to Little Rock." "When I was hauling, I made regular trips to Little Rock," volunteered another, and immediately the conversation moved to favorite and least favorite places.

I am still puzzled. Were they pulling my leg? Did the group know the one who asked the question was a bit weird and knew how to let his questions hang in mid air, unanswered? I don't know.

I took the question home with me. How far can I remember? I remember the Poor. How far is that?

(July)

WELL, I GUESS YOU HEARD that the community of Cherry Log almost disappeared. No, not by wind, fire, or flood, but by a person or persons unknown who probably have never worshiped in Cherry Log, never eaten at the Pink Pig, never attended the free Thursday night music at our community center, probably have no kin buried in our beautiful cemetery.

This person or these persons have the responsibility of preparing from time to time the official map of Georgia. They hold the power of life or death over every village, hamlet, town, or city in the state. One stroke of the pen, one click on the computer, and swoosh, you are gone. This person, or these persons (there must be a group of them, one person could not be so demonic) decided that small communities like Cherry Log are so numerous that they clutter the map, making it difficult for travelers to and through our state to read their maps. So, eliminate Cherry Log and its kind from the map and tourists can more easily find the roads to Atlanta, Savannah, and Augusta.

The camel's nose is in the tent; where will this folly stop? Will the next map have no Valdosta, no Macon, no Marietta? And then the next: will it have no Jasper, no Ellijay, no Blue Ridge, no Blairsville? I see where this is going: finally no Georgia. General Sherman with all his army was not as successful. I urge you to be alert. This mischief is so silent, so creeping, so oozing that it raises no alarm until it is too late. You wake up one morning and where are you? Nowhere. There is no fate so terrible as this, wiped out by the mapmaker.

But cheer up, my friends; I have good news! We have stopped their cold hand. And how? With our documents that prove beyond a shadow of a doubt that rather than Cherry Log confusing the map, it gives purpose and clarity and focus to the map. All those tourists and travelers—they are coming to Cherry Log. According to our documents, without Cherry Log there would be no tourists or travelers to Georgia. So we have not only saved Cherry Log, we have saved Georgia.

We deserve a tax break.

(August)

AN OUTRAGEOUS GIFT. Now and then I am an after-dinner speaker. Such was the case recently at the Home Mission Banquet in Ft. Worth, Texas, during the General Assembly of the Christian Church (Disciples of Christ). We had Texas barbeque. It was not Georgia barbeque, but I kept my mother's instruction, "Clean your plate."

I spoke on "Remember the Poor." I lamented with everyone there the all-too-common themes of downsize, cut back, and reduce programs. Needs, especially of children, increase while funding decreases. In the course of the message I suggested we declare a national Day of Ridiculous Giving. Many of us have boats that are not in the water, a car not being driven, a golf cart or a set of clubs rarely used, an ATV we should not be driving (or a motorcycle, for goodness sake), jewelry we are not wearing, china never taken out of the cabinet, and on and on and on. On an appointed day, why not bring all this to churches or other receiving areas, be rid of a sense of guilt over too much stuff, wait for the announced total (it will be millions), and then enjoy our gifts blessing the poor?

Outrageous? Of course; why not?

At The Craddock Center we have received our first Outrageous Gift. In an envelope on which was the simple message, "Here is my Outrageous Gift," came three beautiful rings. They are wedding rings: two companion rings worn by a bride and a groom's ring. They are bright and beautiful. The woman who sent them offered no story with them. A hundred possibilities, some glad, some sad, come to mind, but I do not know. That is none of my business.

What I have is an Outrageous Gift. The quality of it, the value of it, the beauty of it, the thoughtfulness of it, the many blessings provided by it, move me deeply.

Thank you.

IN CASE YOU ARE FORTUNATE ENOUGH to hit the last traffic light going north on Highway 515 through East Ellijay when that light is red, blessed are you. You will be stopped at Highway 515 and First Street. At that corner, on your right, you will see a beautiful memorial stone marking the site of Fort Hetzel. The inscription is brief and clear. It will tell you that on this site in 1838 stood a fort (really a stockade, a corral) into which were crowded over 1,100 Cherokee Indians, forced into a holding pen until time to begin walking the Trail of Tears to Oklahoma.

If there are small children in your car, read the inscription aloud. If one of them asks you what is a Cherokee, or what is a Trail of Tears, then tell them. They have a right to know; it is part of their heritage.

If the light is green, then you and they will miss it. How unfortunate.

IF I WERE GIVING DIRECTIONS to persons attending the Fall Preaching Workshop, I would not waste their time with reminders of what they already know: the date (October 1), the time (9:00-1:00), and the theme (Preaching a Signature Sermon). I probably would not bring up the free continental breakfast and free deli lunch; who would forget that?

I would speak directly to the question, where is it? It will be in the community room (fellowship hall) of the new Cherry Log Christian Church in beautiful downtown Cherry Log. From the south, go north on Hwy. 515 to mile marker 20, about nine miles north of Ellijay. Turn right at that mile marker onto Cherry Log Street, go about 500 yards to the new blue-gray and white building on the right. From the north, go south on 515 about six miles south of Blue Ridge and at mile marker 20, turn left onto Cherry Log Street. If you are coming from east or west, forget it; no one can travel east and west in Georgia. Lewis and Clark tried it, became lost, and went to the Pacific Northwest instead.

We have plenty of room, but we need your registration. We will have our largest group ever.

(September/October)

YOU WON'T BELIEVE THIS. As I sat here at the Center feeling keenly the difference between what we are doing for the children and what we need to be doing (we simply must enlarge our program), I found myself doing what my father said was useless: wishing. "There is plenty of water in the well," he said, "but you can't wish it to the surface."

Then suddenly I remembered the day I was asked by a man I hardly knew, "Why don't you ask me for money?" "You mean you are asking me to ask you for money?" "That is exactly what I am doing." So, I asked for money from the man who asked me to ask him for money.

And he gave it, and generously, too.

My point is this: Why don't you ask me to ask you for money? We'll see if it works again.

(November)

I MUST BE GETTING SOFT IN MY OLD AGE, but I am beginning to listen to my former students who lament their sad performances in my classes. I enjoy having confessions, but it is beginning to be a bit much.

One recently broke down and said, "If only I could retake the course in preaching," but then he sobbed, "It's too late; what I have written I have written." (This quotation from Pontius Pilate is the only Scripture I ever heard him use.) The women among them seem to be made of sterner stuff; they do not come to the altar.

I know what these preachers want: they want me to unscroll the scroll and change their grades. You see, some have moved into lofty pulpits and in their upward mobility they fear that word of a poor grade may be an impediment. Others have not progressed and blame one bad grade for their stalling out.

So, here's the deal. I will not play favorites; that would be unethical. When I sell grades, I want to be totally fair. For an F to become D, send $100 to The Craddock Center. Likewise for a D to become C, a C to become B, and a B to become A. However, $400 will not make an F an A; that is too big a leap, would look suspicious, and probably raise questions about my fundraising methods. However, the two or three who have across the years received an A are invited to send $400 as an expression of gratitude.

This offer ends as soon as I receive your checks. Hurry; in time some pious soul will cry, "Bribery!" and I don't want any of my old students to be suspected of unethical behavior. The minister's life must be above reproach at all times. Any questions?

(December)

I AM GOING TO VENTURE A GUESS and say that Trisha Senterfitt is going to do a great job as Executive Director of The Craddock Center. I am impressed by her evident care for others, her enthusiasm, her experience and track record in programs serving those in need, and her hard work. I am impressed that she is taking time to know the staff, friends of the Center, past and potential supporters, the community, the network of service organizations, and the needs of those we serve. I am impressed by her deep faith in God and hope for the future.

OK, so Trisha is a Presbyterian. What do you want from me? We advertised the position, conducted an open search, and her name rose quickly to the top. What were we to do? Around the Center several expressed the conviction that God sent her to us. What do you do—send a gift back to God? Besides, I have known several Presbyterians that were decent folk, not bad as neighbors and all that. Very few of us are perfect, and we have to be careful.

Our plan in this: keep Trisha until every Presbyterian in the world has sent a generous donation to our program. Then we will trade her in on an Episcopalian. I'm told those people are loaded.

HAVE I TOLD YOU ABOUT THE VALENTINE BOX? I need to. The fact that it still troubles me is proof enough. Friends who know about such things have long urged me—"Out with it, Fred." The telling may be painful, they say, but the relief that follows is nothing short of pure freedom.

I wanted to. Who knows the number of times that the experience of the Valentine Box rose from the deepest recesses of my memory, reaching my throat but not my lips. I couldn't. I made excuses to myself: this is not the right time, the right place, the right audience.

I am going to. The time, the place, the audience are right. The time is 7:30 p.m., Saturday, January 26, 2008. The place is the Performing Arts Center in Blue Ridge, Georgia. The audience is you, in attendance at our annual evening of Folk Songs and Stories with Steve Darsey and Fred Craddock.

I am going to tell about the Valentine Box. Honest. Cross my heart.

2008

(January)

IS FRED EVER IN THE OFFICE? Well, yes. Why do you ask? I've called twice and he was not there. When did you call? Once I called about 10:00 p.m., and again early in the morning. How early? I don't know; I jog at 6:00 a.m. and it was before that. I can't seem to catch the guy; doesn't he ever work?

I appreciate your frustration. You are one of many victims of his altered schedule. He is now in his office Tuesday, Wednesday, and Thursday, 9:00 till noon. But we can't assure you he is awake. Let the phone ring at least four times. Thanks for asking.

(February)

IN CASE YOU MISSED IT. In Trisha's article last month, we are now taking the Children's Enrichment Program to two additional schools in North Carolina: Ranger and Hiawassee Dam. The teachers urgently requested that we come, and we have. Connie Chancey, one of our Arts Specialists, is taking her enthusiasm and considerable skills to about 48 excited boys and girls.

We cannot, of course, say *Yes* to every request. In fact, you may be wondering why we did in this case since last year we had to cut back due to lack of funds. The answer is simple: we found it easier to work at finding more money than to try to explain to the children why we couldn't come.

Have we found that additional money? Not yet. Any ideas?

I HAVE BEEN IMPRESSED by the amount of time people are saving. It is staggering to contemplate. In some cases the time saved is beyond minutes or hours; it adds up to weeks or months or even years. You do the math: microwave lunch—saves time. Instant coffee—saves time. Send an email—saves time. *Reader's Digest*—saves time. Cliff Notes—saves time. Get a phone/camera/map/directory/radio/pill dispenser/thermometer/rain gauge/Bible concordance/Dial-a-Prayer/first-aid kit all in one, which fits in your wallet—saves time. Use the drive-through window at the funeral home—saves time. When you go fishing, use a fish-finder—saves time. Søren Kierkegaard once told of a man advised by his doctor to take a day off, but the man rested so fast he was finished by noon.

I am certainly no authority on saving time; I have almost used up all my time. In fact, according to the Bible, I am living on borrowed time. Maybe I could have some of the time you have saved. What do you do with it anyway?

Let me warn you: saving time can backfire on you. I know a man who at age 70 had saved a total of 15 years, making him 55, not 70. He lost all his Social Security benefits. So if you are getting anxious about it, stop by (don't email) the Center and we will be glad to take some time off your hands. It's called volunteering, or voling for short—saves time.

(March)

EVIDENTLY **WE HAVE NOT BEEN CLEAR** about who attends Head Start. Last week a person who was just learning of our Children's Enrichment Program asked, "And you take this program to Head Start schools?" "Yes, we do." "Well, isn't Head Start where the children are sent who have learning disabilities; you know, the ones we once called 'retarded'?" "No, absolutely not."

I took this as a "teaching moment" and explained that all schools should provide educational opportunities and programs for those with special needs. Head Start is not different in that regard. But what is different about

Head Start is that it is a pre-kindergarten program for children of the poor. Ninety percent of Head Start children are from families living at or below the poverty level. These children are bright and happy, they respond quickly to stories and songs and rhythmic movement, and, of course, to love and encouragement. If they are lacking, the lack is not in their heads but in their stomachs; not in their hearts but in their homes, often too cold or too hot; not in their potential but in their opportunities. Why not call the Center and arrange a visit to a Head Start school? You'll see.

I probably said a bit more to my questioner, things like how she could serve those who are under-served, etc. You know, essentially what you and I have talked about. Remember?

INTO THE TRASH BARREL—that's where I tossed a file folder containing notes 60 years old. The notes were of my participation on a college debate team. One debate dealt with the role of labor in the management of a company. I argued *for* the proposal but it is evident from my notes that I was pretty much chewed up and spit out by the opposition. Of greater interest was the debate over the resolution that unless an action proceeds from the heart it is not a Christian act. I argued against the proposition.

I am sure supporters of the proposition made a good case: out of a good heart comes the good deed, out of the generous heart comes the generous gift, out of the true heart comes the truth, etc. Who could argue with that? I did.

My point was that we sometimes know what is right to do well in advance of feeling comfortable with it. Racial prejudice, for example. Many people acknowledged what was right long before they felt it in their hearts. The trip from head to heart is often long and painful, but to wait until everyone *felt* right before *doing* right would have been immoral. We can't sit still before a green light waiting until our hearts agree with moving on. The good feeling we want often *follows* rather than *precedes* the action.

The same is true of giving. Suppose one knows a cause or program worthy of a gift; what a shame to wait on sending the gift until the heart is warmly stirred. The good feeling we want is as often the *result* of having given as it is the prompting of the gift. My argument was that actions are Christian not solely because they *come from* the heart but also because they *go to* the heart.

Do you catch my drift? Go ahead and write a check to the Center and if you don't feel good afterwards, I will return your check.

Well, maybe.

(April)

IT HAS BEEN BROUGHT TO MY ATTENTION that I have not yet contributed to the Birthday Fund for the work of the Center. The reminder of my neglect was totally uncalled for. I am very much aware that I have given nothing to the fund. I am the honoree, for goodness sake! The Center is using the occasion of my 80th birthday (April 30) to ask friends and supporters to make a special gift, and, as I understand it, their names will be on a giant birthday card given to me at the appropriate time. I have taken no part in this effort, except to remind two donors that their gifts were not *in memory* of me but *in honor* of me. I'm still here, for goodness sake!

And so I have stayed out of it, so to speak. I must confess that I have once or twice asked Tammy if anyone had sent anything and she reported a generous flow of gifts. For that I am, of course, immensely grateful. But otherwise, I have not intruded myself, confident that such an intrusion would be a gross discourtesy, inappropriate in every way. After all, I am the honoree, for goodness sake!

Wrong, said the reminder. Didn't you grow up in Sunday School? Well, yes, but what has that to do with it? Then you must remember, said my reminder, that in the opening exercises of Sunday School the leader asked if anyone has a birthday that week. If so, while the group sang "Happy Birthday," the birthday boy or girl went to the front and dropped money

46

into a special box, usually in the shape of a church. You see, said my reminder, you learn in church that on your birthday you do not receive; you give.

I stand corrected. I now remember. I also remember from Sunday School that we gave a penny for each year. A ten-year-old would give 10 cents, *et cetera*.

Anyone have change for a dollar?

NETTIE AND I HAVE JUST RETURNED from Emory and Henry College in Virginia where I led a Preaching Workshop. Beautiful country, warm hospitality, a gratifying experience.

On the walls of the room in which the event was held were black and white photos of life in that community in "the good old days." The photos were evidence that the good old days were not so good: tired mules, tired adults, tired children. Appropriate texts accompanied the photos.

Nettie called my attention to the text beside the photo of two young girls, sisters, probably about eight and ten. The text was in the words of the younger who reported the times and ways in which the older sister was "mean to me." Then the older sister became ill with diphtheria. "I knew she was bad sick," wrote the younger, "because she started being nice to me. Just before she died, she gave me a present. She gave me her book."

"She gave me her book." What a sadly beautiful ending to the story.

And what a gift!

(May)

13 WAYS TO END A SERMON is the topic for the Fall Preaching Workshop on October 6, 2008 at Cherry Log Christian Church. Never in the 10 years of offering a Spring and Fall Preaching Workshop at Cherry Log has there been such a swell of interest in a topic—from lay people, listeners to sermons.

"You mean to tell me there are thirteen different ways to end a sermon? Then why in the name of all that is humane and compassionate can't my preacher find one of them?"

"I'm giving my preacher a scholarship to that workshop; how much does it cost?"

"I think my preacher went to a workshop somewhere, but apparently it was on how to end one sermon thirteen times."

"Will the sessions be taped? I want to get a copy for every member of our church and then we'll hold our preacher to it."

"I'm interested in our preacher hearing about those other twelve ways to end. She's been here three years and so far she has ended every sermon the same way."

"Our preacher preaches different. He tells us the ending at the beginning, and then goes on and on and on."

"I don't want my preacher to end her sermon; I could listen for another hour."

The Workshop begins with a continental breakfast at 9:00 a.m. and ends with a deli lunch at 12:00 noon. Everything is free. But all attending need to let us know. We were near our capacity at 140 in March.

I look forward to seeing you.

I'M CHANGING THE WAY I DO BUSINESS, at least some of it. Heretofore, the ways to reach me—mail, email, fax, and phone—have all been through the Center, and these ways have been reasonably satisfactory. However, since I have tried to reduce my time at the Center to Tuesday, Wednesday, and Thursday mornings, some of us are missing each other. Not good.

The fact is, many of you wish to communicate concerning matters unrelated to the work of the Center. These messages are important to me. Messages concerning Center business are important to me also, of course, but our Director, Trisha Senterfitt, and Office Manager, Tammy Blair, are ready and able to respond. Truth be told, even when you contacted me, they were the ones who helped you. It is no longer a secret that I don't know very much.

So, here is my plan. Since much of my reading, writing, and arithmetic is done at home, why not contact me there? By mail, I am at a P.O. box in Blue Ridge, Georgia. By email, out of reach.* My phone was briefly out of service but the repair man welded the crank back on, and it is working fine. I am adding one feature that I think is cutting edge. If I am not in, you can leave a message, and I will call you back. It's called voicemail. Ever hear of it? Awesome. You may ask about a cell phone. Yes, what about it? I went to Wal-Mart to get one of those Blackberries. They didn't have a Blackberry but they had a Prune. Works fairly well, but it's awfully wrinkled.

This new system should be in operation by June 15. I find this new technology rather slow, don't you?

*Editor's Note:
These days, Dr. Craddock **can** be reached by email through the Center: craddockcenter@tds.net

(June)

I AM ASKING YOU to imagine that this is not an issue of *Milk & Honey* but a small card that opens from bottom to top, not from side to side. On the front of the card is a picture of a child in pajamas, kneeling beside a bed, hands together under the chin, eyes closed. Underneath the picture are the words, "*Thank you, God . . .*" You open the card as though lifting a curtain and inside it says,

> "*I thank my God for all your remembrance of me.*"
> *Fred Craddock*

I don't want to be guilty of plagiarism, so I should put beneath these words: The Apostle Paul to the church at Philippi in Macedonia. But at this moment I feel these words are mine. Paul never said to the Philippians, "Thank *you*" but rather "I thank God for you."

I understand what he means, and I also mean it. But I also want to say "Thank *you*." For my eightieth birthday, I received a huge card bearing over 300 names. I also received a big box of notes and letters from you. I have not sat down to read them all at once. Somehow that would seem disrespectful. Rather, I read three or four a day, and I take time to remember you. In addition, the children received from you on my birthday over $61,000. No, this is not a misprint: over $61,000. Every one of these children says, "Thank you."

And, of course, Paul was right. "I thank my God for all your remembrance of me," which, by the way, can also be translated, "I thank my God for all my remembrance of you."

THERE IS A TIME in the evening, between daylight and dark, when the creature population seems to double. The creatures of the day can be seen retreating to their familiar tree or bush or burrow while the creatures of the night cautiously appear from their familiar tree or bush or burrow. For that brief time a field or wood, apparently lacking in creatures, suddenly has more than enough. It is a good time to be alive and awake. Some of my eccentric friends tell me there is a similar drama that unfolds in the morning, early, between night and day. I humor them with a smile, as though I believe it, but they are, as I say, eccentric.

I sat one evening on my front steps, watching the magic of this brief time, when I observed the strangest thing. Down the road (I live on a gravel road, not a street) came walking a nine-pound sparrow. Shocked by the sight of so large a sparrow, I blurted out, "Aren't you a little heavy for a sparrow?" "Why do you think I'm out walking?" he almost yelled. "Why don't you fly?" "Fly? Do you think I'm crazy? I have never flown before!" He walked on, and then it was dark.

2008

(July)

WHILE IT IS TRUE that I am reducing my time at the Center (after all, in Trisha Senterfitt the Center has a strong and capable Director), and that I no longer accept speaking engagements that require plane travel (I do travel by auto, up to 300 miles), it is not true that I am phasing out the Spring and Fall Preaching Workshops at Cherry Log. Of course, a time will come when wisdom says, "Let someone else lead these workshops," but that time is not yet. There are 140+ ministers who will tell me when to turn loose.

And it is not true that this is the last year for the program of Songs and Stories, held every year the last Saturday night in January at the Performing Arts Center in Blue Ridge, Georgia. When Steve Darsey starts telling stories and I start singing, then drop the curtain, it's over.

In the meantime, I am filled with anticipation, and I hope you are.

AS I SAT THE OTHER NIGHT watching the radio, I almost said out loud, "What a technological advance the radio is over the old television!" Oh, the television was okay in its time, but it had so many limitations. For example, the television insisted that you be in the same room with it and staring at it. For what? To watch someone read the news to you, and not nearly as well as radio reporters who were trained to speak clearly and correctly. With the radio, turn up the volume and it reaches into kitchen, bathroom, bedroom, and even barn, in case you haven't finished milking. And TV reporters are poorly treated, being sent "on location" to show us the house in which a death occurred or the highway where a wreck happened earlier. The reporter and camera person, shivering in freezing rain, add nothing to my knowledge. And they have to hurry because, minus the ads, a 30-minute program is 16 minutes. TV must be expensive.

And so much attention is paid to appearances. But not on the radio. Who cared how they looked? In fact, part of the pleasure of radio is imagining whether an announcer or reporter or character in a drama is tall or short, slender or obese, handsome or homely. Sometimes when I meet someone who has heard me but not seen me, he or she may say, "You sounded taller." I like that. I often advised my students in seminary that if they had a chance to be on the radio, take it, but if offered a chance to be on TV, take it only if you have the mental and emotional strength to pretend you are on radio.

But someone says, "Aren't we now in a visual culture?" Well, yes, but in some ways not as much as we have been. For example, a beautiful sanctuary draws the worshiper's eye with tapestry, candle, cross, chalice, table, and banner. It would be a shame to cover all these symbols with a screen that has words on it. Let sights be seen, let words be heard. Good balance.

But for me, nothing comes close to the human voice in a room of listeners.

(August)

MAY I MAKE A CONFESSION? Painful as it is, I must do it.

In the first Scholarship Program for the children, which was so successful thanks to the generosity of so many of you, I did not pledge a scholarship. There, I've said it. Want to shoot me?

I have no excuse. I did not intend such a lapse. Of course, I could try to defend myself with a recital of time given, trips given, speeches given, money given for the overall program, etc., etc., etc., but at the end of it stands the painful fact—I did not give a scholarship. Thirty lashes across my guilty frame! I rejoiced every morning when Tammy opened the mail and there were your gifts. But nothing from Fred. I thanked God for your generosity, but none of mine. I feel like the preacher who urges others on the narrow path that he himself does not take.

Enough of this—I am now taking this public confession to Trisha, our Mother Superior, asking that I be permitted to be the first to pledge a scholarship in the present drive, and a scholarship for the three-year period now past, three years when my soul wandered in waterless places.

No reprimands, please; only grace.

AND IF I AM ELECTED I will push for and sign into law the right of every citizen to carry, concealed or unconcealed as each person may choose, in any public place, a book. Yes, a book. I know this legislation will strike some as too daring and too radical, with unpredictable results. But in countries that already have such a law in place, there is clear evidence that it has proven to be a deterrent to crime, the school dropout rate has fallen, and prisons have overbuilt. If, after 38 years we do not enjoy the same salutary results here, then we can return to the prior state of ignorance, prejudice, and violence.

I am aware that "in any public place" is bold and without restraint, including planes, trains, buses, restaurants, workplaces, hospitals, even houses of worship. But let's try it and see what happens. Sure, books can be dangerous, affecting changes in lives and relationships. Some have done a complete 180 after reading a book. I acknowledge the strong influence of certain books on my life. And we must be warned: some changes are irreversible, but the alternative is frightening. Join me, please, in this bold experiment.

With this bill I will be alerting libraries and bookstores to add to their staffs in order to handle the new rush of business. Likewise, law enforcement personnel will be increased to give order to the crowds. State departments of education will be advised to replace the present exams in math and science with an exam in reading consisting of two questions: Do you have a book? And are you reading it? Churches, social agencies, and faith-based organizations will be called on to supply books to those unable to purchase them. Reading will be taught in all classes, K through college. Reading instruction for adults will be available in every community at night and on weekends.

Be patient with each other; this will take time. If you are on a bus and a person near you pulls out a book and starts reading, don't move to another seat or alert the driver. Just take out your own book, slowly, not hurriedly, and quietly begin to read. Soon everyone will calm down. Oh, someone may interrupt with "What are you reading?" Don't take it as a threat; just answer, "*Abraham Lincoln* by Lord Charnwood; I can't put it down."

(September)

I WAS IN OKLAHOMA when first I heard of an interesting program of the national government to aid farmers, in particular farmers who had been too productive. It seems the law of supply and demand was out of whack due to overproduction of certain commodities, resulting in low prices.

One of the abundant commodities was hogs. A friend of mine was a small-scale hog farmer. The government notified him that he would be paid rather handsomely not to raise any hogs that year. Being patriotic and all, he agreed not to raise his usual 20 hogs. I saw the check. Wow! The program was a success and remained in effect the next year. My friend signed on again, but this time he agreed not to raise 40 hogs. I saw the check. Double wow! The last year he was in the program, he was not raising 200 hogs. I did not see the check. Direct deposit, you know; that much money cannot be trusted to the mail service.

I like this program, more money coming in the less you do. In fact, I am going to try it.

You know about our scholarship program, $140 per year per child in the Children's Enrichment Program. Well, I am not going to mention it.

You know that our Emergency Relief Fund, now near depletion, will face heavy demands with the onset of winter. Well, I will not say a word about it.

You know that we would like to fund another musician/storyteller position so that the lives of more Head Start children can be enriched. Well, I will not bring it up, not even a whisper.

I do like this program. Now every morning I will go to the mailbox full of anticipation.

(October)

MY NEIGHBOR IS DOWN TO ONE ROOSTER and has no hens at all. It is not the economy; it's the hawks, the owls, and one gray fox.

For several years now my farmer neighbor has repaired the hen house, bought hens, and was in business. The rooster crowed, the hens clucked, and chicks chased bugs and grasshoppers. The future looked bright. Then came the hawk and the owl, and chicks disappeared. Then came the fox, and hens disappeared. For three summers the drama repeated itself. Each fall the rooster was alone. This past summer there were no hens or chicks. But there is the rooster.

Now and then he crosses the road to visit me. "Do you still crow?" "Of course; why do you ask?" "Well, I don't see any hens or chicks, so I wondered." "There will be more; my boss is just running late this year; there will be more." The very thought thrilled him. He strutted, flapped, and crowed.

I asked his boss if he were getting more hens. He said no, he couldn't afford to keep doing it. "Have you told the rooster?" "No." "Well, he's hoping." "I know, but I can't take away his hope."

The four-year-old boy who ran into Head Start ahead of me was full of prance and strut. "Did you know my mommy and daddy are buying a car and will pick me up today?" "Wow! That's wonderful!" His mother is a meth addict; his father is in prison.

Did I take away his hope? Did I tell him he had no future? No. In fact, I was there to tell him the opposite, that he *has* a future. Thanks to you.

I CAN'T FIND THE LIST of those who requested of me a copy of a poem I have quoted more than once. As I explained in the speech, I had a calligrapher make two copies that were framed and given to our daughter and son the year she graduated from college and he from high school. I am proud they still have them after more than 30 years. It is a Yiddish poem entitled "Der Ikker" ("The Main Thing").

The poem follows, with the hope that those on the lost list read *Milk & Honey*. To them I apologize. To the rest of you, I give permission to stop reading at this point.

> If your outlook
> on things has changed—
> this is not the main thing.
>
> If you feel like laughing
> at old dreams—
> this is not the main thing.
>
> If you recall errors
> of which you are ashamed—
> this is not the main thing.
>
> Even if you know
> that, what you are doing now,
> you'll regret some other time—
> this is not the main thing either.
>
> But beware lightheartedly
> to conclude from this
> that there is no such thing
> as a main thing—
> this is the main thing.
>
> —*Hirsch Oscherovitch*

2008

(November)

WHEN WE ALL GATHER on Saturday night, January 31, at 7:30 p.m. in the Performing Arts Center of Fannin County High School in Blue Ridge, Georgia, for an evening of songs and stories, I will do my dead-level best to steer clear of tetchy subjects. Not that I am scared, mind you. Just the other day in the barber shop I made my views on Gene Autry plain and clear, let the chips fall where they may.

But feelings in the community about Geraldine are still raw, even though the incident occurred two months ago. The incident is out in the open; it is not unbeknownst to anybody. If you see a huddle of folks, anywhere, anywhen, you know they are talking about Geraldine. The flat-out fact is Geraldine traipsed; there are witnesses. And the witnesses aren't just old women who are so stove up with arthritis they can't traipse anymore and are jealous. Some of Geraldine's friends admit she did it, but they defend her, saying it was a family trait. Geraldine's father lollygagged for years, and an uncle was even arrested for loitering. They say her brother was discharged from the Army for sauntering. You don't saunter off to war.

I didn't see it, but I believe Geraldine traipsed. She's the type. I once heard her ask for a "second serving" of pie instead of a "second helping" like the rest of us. And they say she has in her bedroom a chiffonier.

Traipsing is bad enough but get this: she traipsed into prayer meeting. Into prayer meeting! You don't traipse into prayer meeting any more than you traipse into a funeral home. My land of living, is nothing sacred anymore?

She'll be churched, for sure.

FOR WHAT IT'S WORTH I have increasing respect for ministers I meet, especially the younger ones, male and female, lay or ordained. And I have met thousands since retiring from the seminary classroom in 1993. We meet in workshops and seminars, in their parishes, and around the big table at The Craddock Center.

I have no theory about this. Maybe part of this perception lies in me, now that I have tossed the grade book, gotten old, and maybe softened a bit. But I really do believe the quality is rising. Sure, there is here and there the lazy one, and sure, there is here and there the egotist, needing tons of attention, always high maintenance. And we all know that, like medical doctors, not all ministers made straight A's in school. Even so, the general impression is positive.

And in what ways? My exposure to them is limited, of course, but I sense more passion in the work, more willingness to learn and improve, more discipline in study, more courage in witnessing, and more attention to their relationship to God. This relationship to God is not some self-caressing indulgence in a vague cloud of spirituality. Rather it is active, enquiring, discerning, and demanding. In ways formal and informal, such a minister enables me in my own longing to know God. Such a minister has an altar in every sermon, whatever its form and style.

I will not name names. You already have thought of someone, perhaps your own minister.

(December)

I AM EXPECTING a larger crowd than usual for "Winged for the Heart," the program of songs and stories that Dr. Steve Darsey and I present each year on the last Saturday night in January. That will be January 31, at 7:30 p.m. Not that we haven't had good attendance every year; we have, averaging well over 400.

But this year the crowd will be noticeably larger. Not because of the weather, although it will be a beautiful night—cool but not cold, clear sky, full moon, a million stars, Big Dipper and Little Dipper so close you think you can reach up and touch them. Probably some will be asking to have the program outside, and we would, but the sound equipment fellows say the night air is hard on their equipment. We best stay inside.

And I have to confess it will not be the program itself that swells the crowd, although interest is rising. Word is out that my introductory comments will be on Adverbs. Yes, Adverbs. I don't know how it is where you live, but around here the interest in Adverbs is near epidemic. I have succumbed to the pressure. I will, of course, tell those present about the Man Made of Adverbs, totally of Adverbs; not a noun or verb in his body, not even a preposition.

The fact is multitudes will come because of the economy. You see, our program is free, and right now people are looking for free. Sure, we take an offering, but you've been in church enough to know how to handle the offering: fumble in your pockets until the basket moves on.

Did I mention we begin at 7:30?

2009

THE FACT THAT I AM DOING NOTHING does not mean that nothing is being done. On the contrary, there is now more activity at The Craddock Center than at any time previously. Dr. Trisha Senterfitt is a strong, hard-working, and imaginative Director. Tammy Blair is an amazing Office Manager; a quick learner, with an eye for detail, of unwavering loyalty, and always welcoming. The Center Board is now at full strength and participating in the program.

And speaking of the program, more children are being served and in more ways. For example, this month a grief program for children who have lost a family member will begin. The Story Express has delivered more books than ever. We have a stronger than ever network with other agencies that serve the poor. Regularly scheduled programs (Helen Lewis Lecture, Songs and Stories, Preaching Workshops, Appalachian Weekend) continue to grow in numbers and support. More volunteers are showing up. In short, 2008 was a great year.

So don't let my doing nothing fool you. Rather, expect an even greater year in 2009 because I will do even less. The only persons doing less are the deceased. Don't get me wrong: I will continue the Preaching Workshops and the Songs and Stories, but I will absent myself from daily operations. I will spend less time at the Center. If I am needed, Tammy will call me, and if any of you wish to talk with me, I am at home. I have no email address, but at home I will answer, Nettie will answer, or the voicemail will answer.*

And the reason for this slackening on my part? I could say it is because I have three writing projects underway, but the real reason is that in 20 years I will be 100 years old. Give me a break!

*Editor's Note:
If Dr. Craddock is needed, please email him through the Center: craddockcenter@tds.net. We'll make sure he gets your message.

I HOPE YOU DON'T MIND that I have asked Steve (Darsey) to include a couple of Appalachian hymns in his repertoire for the Songs and Stories program on Saturday night, January 31. Of course, those who know Appalachian culture can hear the faith of the people in most of the songs, whether they are about train workers, mine explosions, jealous husbands, or coon dogs. But some songs were written to be sung in religious gatherings: church worship, funerals, or camp meetings. In fact, a few have made their way into church hymnals and are often sung with appreciation by folk with no Appalachian memory.

OK? Good; I felt you would agree. After all, Appalachian culture, like any oral culture, is passed along by old sayings, stories, and songs, including songs of faith.

I look forward to seeing you on Saturday night, January 31, at 7:30, in the Performing Arts Center on the campus of the Fannin County High School in Blue Ridge.

(February)

IT IS NO COINCIDENCE that at the Spring Preaching Workshop on Monday, March 2, Dr. Jennie Perryman will join us to present a lecture. The theme for the morning is "Preaching the End Time" and her after-lunch lecture will deal will End-of-Life Care. It is a subject on which Dr.

Perryman is well qualified, both by study and by passion. Her current position is in the Organ Transplant Unit of Emory Hospital. The morning and afternoon discussions deal with ministry in and out of the pulpit.

So—are we clear? Dr. Craddock will deal with "Preaching the End Time" during the morning; after a complimentary lunch ending about 12:45, Dr. Perryman will present. It is our hope that everyone attending the morning session will remain through the early afternoon. Since the number of lunches prepared will be affected, please let Tammy know (phone or email) your plans.

I know I will stay. In my own preparation for ministry, End-of-Life Care was all too briefly treated. We are grateful in advance to Dr. Perryman.

I LEARNED JUST RECENTLY of a case of surgery so extraordinary that I assumed it was a singular case, but the surgeon assured me it was not. Rare, yes, but unique, no.

The story in brief is this: a man in his mid-fifties was rushed to the emergency room of the nearest hospital. He complained of inability to breathe. Examination revealed that the cause of his shortness of breath was a growth, a large growth, on his upper back, between his shoulder blades. The man's mother said she first noticed it when he was a teenager. She repeatedly urged him to have it attended to, but he never did. The growth was small when she first noticed it, and on subsequent occasions she could tell it was growing. Her urgings moved from cosmetic (it was becoming unsightly) to medical (it will put pressure on your heart). When her son became an adult and moved away, she worried but did nothing more. The patient himself gasped to the doctor that the growth had enlarged very gradually and had been accepted as a part of his life. He grew unable to imagine himself without it; it became a part of his identity. It caused little or no pain; that is, until recently.

The growth had to be removed; there was no alternative to surgery. A team of surgeons was assembled. They began at 7:00 a.m. and finished at

3:30 p.m. One or two follow-up surgeries might be required, but the patient would live. Barring unexpected complications, he should enjoy a life free of unnecessary weight; a new life, one might say.

How much did the growth weigh? Everyone was curious to know. Slightly more than 40 pounds. How in the world was he able to carry it, day and night? Because it grew so slowly. Would it have been fatal if not removed? No question. Was it sent to the lab for analysis? Of course, it always is. What was it?

A grudge.

(March)

I AM ALREADY AT WORK on the Fall Preaching Workshop scheduled for October 5, 2009. Why begin so far in advance? The reasons are two: one, the importance of the subject matter; two, the complexity of the subject matter.

We will be discussing "Emotion in Preaching." Certainly emotion is much more than feeling, even though it includes feeling. And shall we locate it in the preacher or in the listener? If we say, "In both," then does emotion flow from one to the other? If so, then are we not into manipulation? Would it not be better to avoid emotion altogether simply to avoid its misuse, as in "Emotionalism"? But the fact is, emotion in communication cannot be avoided, unless, of course, it is a case of the dead talking to the dead. At best, what we can hope for is genuine rather than manufactured emotion. Can *you* tell the difference?

Woe is me! I have only seven months to prepare.

Is it too late to change the subject?

Yes.

REFLECTIONS ON MISSING APPOINTMENTS DUE TO ILLNESS. I have had to miss five speaking engagements in recent weeks due to illness, and I want you to be my confessor because I feel guilty. Yes, guilty, and I don't know why.

I would understand the feelings of guilt if I had at the last minute been invited on a cruise or been offered a cottage on the sand and had my secretary send five "Sorry, I'm sick" notes. But no cruise or cottage here.

Or the guilt feelings would be appropriate if I had dilly-dallied, failed to prepare adequately, and called in sick. You remember, don't you, the homework was not done so, "Momma, I have a stomachache." Not the case here; five speeches lie here on my desk.

I would even accept the feelings of guilt if my illness were borderline; you know, don't really feel up to it but with aspirin I could probably make it. Getting up and going under such a circumstance would have its rewards. "Even though I was sick, I preached" has a nice ring to it. Martyr like. But this illness was not borderline. I had pneumonia, for crying out loud! Even when I was paralyzed with Guillain-Barré Syndrome and had to cancel my classes, I felt guilty. When I lay in North Fulton Hospital, split open like a slaughtered hog, following a botched colonoscopy, I missed several Sundays in the pulpit, and—you guessed it—I felt guilty.

What do you think is my problem? Maybe I have taken "In spite of dungeon, fire, and sword" too literally. Maybe I have let the Apostle Paul set the bar too high: "It was because of my illness I preached to you the first time." Maybe it is ego, plain and simple, thinking myself so necessary for an event that no substitute, no postponement, no program change will work. Maybe it is just poor planning. When saying "Yes" to an invitation, throw in four or five "ifs"; then I'm covered in advance. I do know that those friends who speak knowingly of God's will or who recite Paul's "Satan has hindered me" have not erased the feelings of guilt.

It could be the case that I am too concerned about what my would-be hosts might think of me. During my illness, when Nettie answered the phone, I comforted myself with the thought, "They are saying, 'He's really sick; the poor dude can't even answer his phone.'" But when she ran an errand, I picked up the phone and could almost hear, "He doesn't sound all that sick."

If you know what's wrong with me, don't tell me. I have lived so long with questions I am more comfortable with them than with answers.

In the meantime, I'm walking around with five undelivered speeches inside me. I feel a headache coming on.

(April)

LET ME RECOMMEND that you spend some time now and then remembering your childhood, from your earliest recollection through elementary school years. Retrieve from your memory how you dressed, what you ate, what you played and with whom, your room, your siblings, your parents, going to church, teachers you loved and why, teachers you feared and why, what made you happy, what made you sad, what you wanted to be when you grew up. You get the idea. Revisit specific persons, places, events.

Why do this? There may be some pain in it. Of course, there may be, but you will understand better why you are as you are. Better self-understanding makes possible better understanding of others and with that more patience, more kindness, more gratitude. In fact, you may be more comfortable saying *Yes* to invitations to serve others, especially children who will someday remember you with fondness and gratitude.

At The Craddock Center we believe strongly that attention and encouragement from one adult outside the family make a major difference in the life of a child.

Remember?

IT IS DIFFICULT TO BELIEVE that our Fall Preaching Workshop on October 5 will be the twenty-fifth. Think of it: 25 workshops together! There was only one in 1997, held in the little pavilion on Bear Lake. Perhaps as many as twenty attended, ministers from nearby. In 1998, two were held, spring and fall, again in the pavilion. In 1999, the Spring Workshop was in the pavilion, the Fall Workshop in the new church building on the hill. Attendance grew to the capacity of that building, about 100 around tables. Now in the new Cherry Log Christian Church building, the community room accommodates about 150. We have already tested that capacity, but that's it; we are not going to start a second layer, nor are we going to separate attendees by age, gender, experience, size, or velocity. I enjoy the mix, and as long as you are there, all is well.

As we approach our twenty-fifth, several impressions hold my attention:

- Most ministers honor the pulpit and take preaching seriously.
- Around the pulpit preachers can gather, young and old, experienced and inexperienced, male and female. I saw a minister from a denomination that forbids women in the pulpit embrace a female participant.
- Mutual support and encouragement are priceless, especially in a time when many ministers are taking a beating.

I look forward to seeing you October 5. Be sure you are registered; we may be crowded. We are going to discuss genuine and non-genuine emotion in preaching: "Once More With Feeling." I am already feeling good.

(May)

I STOPPED THE OTHER DAY FOR A TRAIN. It was at the Maxwell Road crossing. I was on my way home. As you know, I live across the tracks.

I was in no hurry. I grow impatient with automobiles, and with pedestrians, but not with trains. Trains take precedence not only by size but also by seniority. And by respect. Trains were here long before automobiles. Trains don't cut corners, dart in front of you, cut you off, jay walk, or stand like a statue in the middle of the street. Trains stay on track.

I have never seen an obscene gesture by a train engineer or by a brakeman. Train workers wave, even to children, especially to children. I didn't get a wave from the engineer the other day; the engine was already

50 yards down the track when I arrived at the crossing. And no wave from the brakeman on the caboose; there was no caboose. I was saddened by no caboose; the train seemed incomplete. Maybe it is the recession. I hope not. Let the recession hit business, builders, and banks, but not take the caboose. I spent my childhood in the Great Depression and every train kept its caboose.

Some are saying trains are making a comeback. If so, I hope it is not in a flurried hurry. If in a hurry, trains will probably carry passengers; in other words, riding pedestrians with an attitude. And probably haul automobiles, arrogant and rude. Then I will probably lose my temper and try to cross ahead of the train, and be killed by the train.

I don't want that on my marker: "Killed by a train"—by a rude motorist maybe; by an irate pedestrian maybe. But not by a train. I love the train.

WHAT ARE THE ODDS? That was the question put to the trainer of Mine That Bird, a bay gelding from New Mexico, now stalled at Churchill Downs, and waiting.

"I don't think in terms of odds."

"But you must be aware that your horse is a long shot."

"Yes, but as long as we have a shot."

"The numbers I am hearing are 50 to 1."

"All we ask is a chance to compete."

- - - -

What are the odds?

That was the question asked as we stood outside the door of the Head Start school.

"I don't think in terms of odds."

"But you must be aware that these children are a long shot to survive their social and economic disadvantages, stay in school, and become productive citizens."

"Yes, but as long as they have a shot."

"The numbers I am hearing are 50 to 1."

Just then a young woman full of energy, good cheer, and love for children entered the room. Faces lit up as the children gathered for their good morning hugs. Then they listened, sang, danced, and sat in a circle to hear their names and receive a book, a new book of their very own.

"What were the numbers you heard?"

"50 to 1."

"Oh, you must be thinking about horses, not these children."

(June)

I THOUGHT YOU MIGHT LIKE TO KNOW how I can be reached now that I am at the Center less frequently and less predictably. My home phone number remains the same. I would be pleased to talk with you. If you call when I am napping (I sleep well at night and fairly well in the morning, but in the afternoon I just toss and turn), leave a message on the voicemail. I have a new mailing address in Cherry Log, Georgia.* We had a box at the Blue Ridge Post Office, but in July Blue Ridge will have a new post office, at least a mile more distant than the present one. We really should have had a Cherry Log box all along, but it's water over the dam, so to speak.

If you continue to send gifts to the Center, and surely you will, please do not send them to my box. Gifts sent to me will, within the hour, become ice cream and peanut butter. Tammy will inform me from time to time who has given to the Center and that will give me an excuse to call or write you.

In the meantime, I will be occupied with my new business: a small roadside shack trafficking in fish bait, boiled peanuts, and services such as motorcycle repair and acupuncture.

Editor's Note:
Please continue to send notes to Dr. Craddock through the Center:
craddockcenter@tds.net

TARNATION. I have just returned from Chattanooga where a retirement service was held for the word "Tarnation." We could see retirement coming; sometimes a week will pass without hearing Tarnation. Some of us tried to delay retirement by using the word in public places at least once every day. Puzzled looks told us—it is time for it to go.

But there was a time when Tarnation flourished as though it would live forever. And it was so useful, in the home, at school, in the pulpit. I can hear it now: Where in tarnation do you think you are going? Why in tarnation are you wearing that? How in tarnation do you expect to get home? It wasn't necessary to know what the word meant; it accomplished the purpose wherewith it was spoken. The scholars who read this newsletter (and there are many) would, of course, expect a definition, so for your sake here it is.

Tarnation is the union of "tarnal" and "damnation." Tarnal is a common mispronunciation of Eternal. Damnation you already understand. Put the two words together, abbreviate, and you have Tarnation. As you have probably guessed, the word provides a way for Christians to cuss without cussing (I use "cuss" in the widely popular sense to cover swearing, cussing, taking God's name in vain, and general profanity). Christians don't hold to cussing, but sometimes they need to in the worst way. So they developed this clever way of almost cussing. For instance, "Darn," or "Gosh," or "For land's sake," or "By golly," or "Goodness gracious."

But no expression exceeds Tarnation, in beauty or power or general usefulness.

We had a good crowd in Chattanooga, well-behaved and respectful. Oh, there were a few protestors and a smattering of the curious. One of these curious passersby almost boastfully told me he never heard the word. "Never heard it?" I replied. "Where in Tarnation have you been?"

(July)

YES, I GUESS YOU COULD SAY that our Children's Enrichment Program adds luxury to the otherwise rather sparse lives of many of the children we serve. This is not to say that we regard as of less value the basic needs of food, clothing, and shelter, needs that occupy parents of the children. Of course not. We watch and listen and often stretch our funds to help address those needs. But the point is, we do not regard all luxuries as luxuries. A story, a song, a book, a toy, a funny hat, a silly game: these, too, are necessities, not luxuries. It is not the case that bread on the table is the only necessity; so is the candle, the violin, the colorful napkin, and the laughter of those who love the child. These, too, are essential because the children are human beings, created in God's image, with hearts, minds, feelings, and imagination.

Once Jesus and his friends were guests at a dinner party at which a woman anointed Jesus with an expensive ointment. Some of Jesus' friends objected, calling her act "wasteful." Jesus heard their complaining and responded sharply, "Leave her alone; she has done a beautiful thing for me."

I'm sure you already know, but let me again assure all you who give to the Children's Enrichment Program: Not one penny of your gift is wasted. Every penny goes toward those things every child *really needs.*

Thank you for your generosity.

I'M LOOKING FORWARD to October 5. As you know, that is the day when we gather for the Fall Preaching Workshop. I always anticipate these workshops: the conversations, seeing old friends and new, thinking and talking preaching, the relaxed "Preachers Day Out" atmosphere.

But this fall my anticipation is keener, and I'm not sure why. This will be the twenty-fifth workshop, but that hardly accounts for the edge to my expectation. Meeting twenty-five times could just as easily dull one's appetite as sharpen it. I am, of course, drawing nearer the close of my work as teacher and preacher, but the approach of the end of activities filled with pleasure and gratitude hardly quickens one's spirit. The closing out of other activities probably leaves me with more energy for this, which may be a factor in my accelerated anticipation. Maybe.

But my guess is that the subject, the theme for this workshop, accounts for my quickening pulse. I have offered as a title "Once More with Feeling." A subtitle might be "Emotion in Preaching: Genuine or Manufactured?" A brief summary of our discussion would include several important matters: Are we talking about manipulation of feelings in ourselves and in listeners? Can we, or should we, trust feelings? Doesn't emotion involve more than feeling? Is not "knowing" better than "feeling"? Should we not trust the message to do its own work apart from our feelings or those of our listeners? If there is, as often reported, a decline of passion in preaching, how can one account for it? Has the busyness, the haste, the shallowness of life in our culture robbed preachers of the time and even the motivation to think and to feel?

But wait; I get ahead of myself. I told you my expectation is high, my anticipation keen.

I hope you will join me October 5.

(August)

WHEN IS THE LAST NOT THE LAST? You know the answer: When the leader of a program ceases to lead but the program goes on.

For example: On October 5 of this year, I will hold my last session of the Fall Preaching Workshop at Cherry Log. Counting both Spring and Fall Workshops, this will be the twenty-fifth. The theme is "Emotion in Preaching" and I look forward to our time together.

But what is of prime importance is that the workshop will continue on its present schedule and with strong leadership. Trisha has already secured unusually capable leaders for 2010, both spring and fall.

Last week I was asked by a minister from out of state and coming this fall for the first time whether I would be leading the workshop. When I said "Yes," he continued, "But isn't your leadership of the program at its end?" I said, "Nearabout." He said, "What?" I repeated "Nearabout." Poor fellow obviously struggling with the English language. What will he do with roundabout, hereabout, turnabout, or whereabout? I'll probably have to explain to him what the workshop is *about*.

IT LOOKS LIKE WE WILL BE ABLE to increase our Children's Enrichment Program this fall, at least that is the news I get from Trisha: Another musician/storyteller for Head Start children. I hope, I hope, I hope.

Those Head Start children have no idea what a treat is in store for them. That is, if the new member of the team is anything like the ones we already have. Have you met them? They are excited and exciting, full of love for children, talented, self-giving, and prepared. When they walk into a room, everyone knows someone just came in and the room is already different.

I read somewhere that if a child, even a child in poverty and neglect, has one adult outside the family who is caring and encouraging, that child's chances of remaining in school and succeeding in life rise sharply. I know that one adult, and I predict that 25 years from now lawyers, doctors, ministers, teachers, good mothers and fathers will stop by the old Head Start school looking for that person who made the difference, just to say "Thank you." I know it will happen. In fact, some of the parents of these children are already, in advance, saying "Thank you."

Even those of you not parents of preschoolers are probably now thinking of some way to join in the "Thank you."

(September)

EMPTY YOUR POCKETS. When I remembered those words I shuddered as though a possum had run over my grave. The security guard probably thought he was the cause of my apparent anxiety, but he was not. Airport security is child's play compared to the drill of Miss Fannie Harris, principal of the grammar school where I was a second grader.

Someone had shot off a firecracker on the playground at recess. Miss Harris went on alert. Who brought firecrackers to school? Boys were summoned to her office. Not all boys; only the usual suspects. Why I was among them remains a mystery to me.

"Empty your pockets," she said, and we did. I began by rather selectively placing on her desk the objects that constituted my identity as a human being. First a yellow pencil; I thought to impress her with my scholarship. She was not impressed. Next a pocketknife, proof of my manhood, but my trembling gave me away. Then my magnifying glass. She had no clue what a powerful weapon it was. Held one way, the glass magnified; held another, it intensified, drawing the rays of the sun to a hot point, burning paper, or someone's arm. Poor Miss Harris, she never even suspected. Next, my marbles, three of them, and beautiful, the color of butter and molasses. She didn't even touch them, out of respect, I guess. Marbles were as good as money. "I would throw that away," she said, looking at my rabbit's foot. "There's no such thing as luck, good or bad." I did not respond, but I figured if it will get me out of this mess I will carry it forever. "And that, too" she said, referring to my half-eaten cookie. True, it was soiled and had gathered a bit of lint, but you have to leave it unwrapped for easy access during class. "Well, I never" was all she said about my chicken foot. Obviously she had never heard the girls go screaming when I sneaked up on them and pulled the tendon that made the toes move. That foot was the envy of the town boys. As to my ball of string, no comment. Everybody carries string; that is, everybody with any religion at all. Miss Harris knew what I know, and you know, that string was the first thing God created. How else could God hang the sun and moon and stars? "Is that all?" "Yes, ma'm." "You may go." I did.

No firecrackers.

I learned later that one of the older students (a third grader) confessed to shooting the firecracker, but the confession was not accepted. You see, the one confessing was a girl, and in those days there was a lot of prejudice against girls. They never got credit for a lot of the fun stuff that happened at school.

(October)

IT IS QUITE UNDERSTANDABLE that the Center be concerned about my retirement. It is not personal; I am still welcome to hang out now and then, as long as I stay out of the way of those who have work to do. In other words, life around the Center is as it has always been for me. Rather, the concern is financial. After all, a considerable portion of our income came from my preaching and teaching with the honoraria going to the Center. How will that lack be supplied?

No problem. The plan is simple: churches and other groups will be asked to pay for my *not* coming to them to preach or teach. A simple note accompanying your check will suffice to enable Tammy to keep clear financial records. For example, "Dr. Craddock did not show up for our Homecoming, and in appreciation enclosed is a check to the Center for $500." Or perhaps, "Dr. Craddock has never been to our church and in gratitude we are sending $750." Or again, "This is the seventh year in a row Dr. Craddock has not been here. Please accept our gift of $700. In the future, for each year he fails to show we will increase our gift $100." Or this: "Our church is growing, not in spite of but because of Dr. Craddock's absence. Enclosed find a check for $1,000." One more possibility: "We have no plans to invite Dr. Craddock to our church and that bright prospect has moved our Board to unprecedented generosity. Celebrate with us by receiving our check for $2,000."

Are you following me? Good. Tammy will keep a separate record of gifts to the Un-Craddock Fund (or perhaps, the Silence is Golden Fund). From time to time we will publish in the *Milk & Honey* newsletter some of the more clever notes along with the amounts given. And, of course, you will be informed about the totals given.

You will notice that I have not increased my usual honoraria, although some will likely find that my absence was more valuable than my presence. I simply feel that I should not take advantage of churches by getting greedy in my absence. I realize there are many capable preachers and teachers who will not come to your church for less. But let me just say that if you never see me again, we are grateful for your generosity. Especially if it comes to us annually. And if I should, by some fluke of scheduling, show up in your community, your check will be returned along with an apology from me.

Frankly, I see nothing but happy days ahead.

(November)

I AM SITTING HERE trying to think of a way to use the word "unbeknownst" in an article I am writing. I like the word; it's from a good family: an English mother and a German father.

I'm not having much luck. Maybe a lack of oxygen to the brain. I am very aware of oxygen lately. Recovering from pneumonia, I have been on oxygen. And I must confess being in a foul mood about it. I wanted to blame my neighbor for breathing too much, but I couldn't; they are barely breathing. It's the trees, I thought. Their job is to take in carbon dioxide and give off oxygen. We live in the middle of a woods and there are only two of us, for goodness sake! I threatened to replace the trees with cactus until one smart-leafed young poplar reminded me that we were not the only animals in the forest.

So—I've been on oxygen. It's not free by a long shot. Just like water. Not any more. Where is Al Gore when you need him?

When the technician came with the oxygen machine, he asked me how long a hose I needed. I told him 14 miles; 12 miles to Wal-Mart and 2 looking for the bottled water. It's cheaper to go to church; only 3 miles. He assured me they would service the hose to guard against people tapping into it. Good. Down the road is a family from Chicago, and those people are famous for breathing other folks' oxygen.

The oxygen man just left. My oxygen is normal again. I have apologized to the family from Chicago and thanked the trees.

A word of advice: check your oxygen. There is an invisible drama being played out, totally unbeknownst to you.

(December)

I'LL BET I'VE TOLD TRISHA one hundred times that there is no need for me to write this article. And one hundred and one times she has said that I need to write it. It is only natural, she says, that some supporters of our program may wonder if my retirement creates any uncertainty about the future of our mission. So why not, she repeats, a few sentences from you to the effect that your retirement does not alter our program or mission in the least?

But, Trisha, the program *is* altered already.

She is shocked. How so?

Under your leadership the Center Board is larger, stronger, and more committed; the Children's Enrichment Program serves more children; the number of singers and storytellers has increased; more volunteers have been enlisted; more books and toys have been received and given away; we have wider name recognition than ever—shall I go on?

But longtime supporters as well as new ones need to have clear assurance that there will be no change of direction, that our program and mission remain the same. That is a commitment.

Trisha, be not anxious. Let's make a deal. If in the next 12 months there is any drop-off of support, even one nickel; no, let's say it more strongly: if there is not an increase in gifts, then I will admit I was wrong. But if there is no drop-off but rather an increase in support, then you will admit you were wrong.

Agreed?

Agreed.

Now, my friends, prove me right. All the children are cheering for me, hoping I am right. In fact, I think deep down Trisha is hoping I am right. But will she admit it? We'll see.

2010

THE BARN IS NOW GONE, but the story continues. The barn looked like dozens of other barns in southern Ohio: shelter for animals, stalls for milking, safe places for newborn calves. Storage for harness and tools, and a loft for hay. It was the loft that set this barn apart.

One summer day a teenage boy stopped at the farm looking for food and shelter. "I don't ask for wages; I'll work for my food and I'll sleep in the barn." It was agreed. And so every evening after supper, the boy climbed up into the loft. There he slept and dreamed of a future, determined not to be denied a future simply because he was poor. One evening, lying in the hay and waiting for sleep to come, he took out his pocketknife and carved his initials on the rafter overhead.

I don't know how long he worked there, nor do I know how many years passed before the farmer noticed the carving. Nor do I know when and by whom the section of rafter containing the carved initials was carefully removed and taken away. I do know the initials: J.A.G., James A. Garfield, twentieth president of the United States.

Soon you should begin to check your barn lofts. You see, there are graduates of Head Start and our Children's Enrichment Program who are now 13 years old. One of them may stop by your place looking for work, any kind of work. If you can, say *Yes,* but even if you can't, he or she will move on, determined not to be denied a future simply because they are poor.

2010

(February)

IF YOU ARE NOT A PREACHER, I suggest you contact Trisha in the Center office to find out if you can attend the Spring Preaching Workshop on March 1. Her response, I am sure, will be based entirely on space available. At the Fall Workshop there were 180. We were packed. It worked out acoustically, but some complained about the awkwardness of eating lunch in the balcony, since we have no balcony.

It is understandable that non-preachers would want to attend, given the unusual nature of the program. Our leader for the day, Dr. Eugene Lowry, is not only a proven teacher of preaching, but he is also a gifted jazz pianist. And the unique feature is that he joins the two. He will demonstrate the kinship between improvisation in jazz and in preaching. This is our first opportunity to promote a workshop that has both entertainment and education value.

My own estimation of a teacher begins with the matter of whether or not the teacher gives his or her best to every audience. Some teachers give freshmen the same tired old notes and give graduate students their newest and best thoughts. Some preachers save for the tall steeple their best sermon, but rush off to the small church with leftovers.

Not so, Dr. Lowry. He was recently at Yale University and now he comes to Cherry Log. There will be no drop-off in quality of material or in respect for his audience. So … call Trisha.

(March)

I HAVE NO IDEA why I've been thinking a good deal lately about Eleanor Roosevelt. Why Eleanor and not Franklin? If it were Franklin, I could account for my thinking by the fact of our recent celebration (February 15) of Presidents Day. But the fact is, on February 15, I didn't think of F.D.R. or any other president. On February 12, I remembered President Lincoln and recited again his Gettysburg Address. On February 22, I remembered President Washington, and read again his Farewell Address to the Troops.

I do not associate February 15 with any president, and certainly not with any president's wife.

This is not to take lightly the wives of presidents. On the contrary, many of them have been persons of grace and strength who brought honor to the White House. And most certainly, I do not regard lightly Eleanor Roosevelt. In my judgment she was the most extraordinary of all the First Ladies. She gave her voice and her presence to the poor, to endeavors that brought on her widespread criticism. My own father voted for Franklin but wanted him to leave Eleanor at home. My mother praised Eleanor's brave efforts.

But this is ancient history. Sixty-five years ago Eleanor Roosevelt carried her husband's corpse from the Capital. I was 17 years old—a long time ago.

So, why am I thinking of her? Your guess is as good as mine. I know we sometimes wake in the morning with the memory of an event or a person vivid and clear. Or we wake with a tune playing in our heads and it refuses to go away. It is probably wise, rather than trying to chase away the image or silencing the tune, to embrace the image, to hum the song, let them enrich the day and then let them retire to the shades of forgetfulness.

And so I said to Eleanor, "Say something so that I can move on past this uninvited memory." And Eleanor Roosevelt said, "No one can make you feel inferior without your permission."

Now I don't think I will ever forget.

(April)

SHARPER THAN THE PAINS to body, mind, and spirit that all of us endure in our lifetime are the pains we feel when our children are hurt. And they do get hurt, even when being the objects of our most careful attention. Life can seem so uneven and so unfair.

I have in mind now not the cut finger or the sudden fever, but the blows to the mind and to the heart. The parent fears the lingering effects of hurt feelings or of a sense of being wronged by some person or event. No parent wants a son or daughter to carry into adulthood a sense of being a victim, or perhaps worse, a veiled hostility that wants to get even.

It was my mother's habit to dull her children's pain and even to rise above the cause of hurt by creating out of the occasion a song. An example. One morning she returned to the kitchen from the smokehouse, knife in hand but with no ham. Hams were smoked in a small out building to which Momma went on wintry mornings to retrieve slices of ham to feed her brood. But in the night someone had stolen the ham. She had her own pain, but she felt ours as well. No ham! "He's going to the Bad Place when he dies, isn't he, Momma?"

Momma was at the stove, busy but silent. In a few minutes she began to hum. She was writing a song in her head. Then she began to sing:

> We have biscuits, we have jam;
> Let him have that greasy old ham.
> How can he eat that greasy old ham,
> When we have the biscuits and we have the jam?

The tune was light and easy. Soon we were all singing, smearing jam on biscuits and feeling a bit sorry for the man who was left with that greasy old ham.

(May)

THERE IS A RIGHT WAY to make introductions of persons to each other, and she did it right. "Jeffrey, this is Fred; Fred, this is Jeffrey." Jeffrey and I shook hands. "Hi, Jeffrey"; "Hi, Fred." The "she" was Janice, Jeffrey's mother.

But if the social amenities were so right, why my slight but perhaps noticeable reaction? I don't know. I see Jeffrey now and then and it's "Hi, Jeffrey"; "Hi, Fred." I think my reaction, ever so slight, was prompted by the fact that I am 82 years old and Jeffrey is 5. I am quite comfortable saying "Hi, Jeffrey" but how can he be so comfortable saying "Hi, Fred"?

Did I mention that I am 82 and Jeffrey is 5? I baptized his grandmother, for crying out loud! Five years ago Jeffrey was but a kick in his mother's womb while I was out saving the world. Surely that counts for something. Of course, there is something I like about Jeffrey calling me Fred: he is comfortable around me; he accepts me in spite of my age and many infirmities; he is at ease in a world of adults; we are in many ways alike.

So, what's my problem? In the world of my growing up, a child never called an adult by his or her first name. It was Miss or Mrs. or Mr. To this day, when I greet a former teacher, it is Miss Jessie, Miss Jane, Mr. Gray, Mr. Thomas. I still cannot call former seminary professors Steve, or Edwin, or Phil. Even in graduate school, on one of my more adult days, I referred to a professor as Lee and an older faculty member said, "Are you referring to Dr. Keck?" The old reprimand was still alive: "Respect your elders."

My son is right: "No disrespect is intended, but it's a new day and a new age." And I'm pleased to report that I am growing more accustomed to this new day. By the time I am 90, I'll be cool with it.

I saw Jeffrey the other day. "Want to play some video games?" he asked. "I don't know how." "It's okay; I'll teach you."

(June)

AT THE CENTER, WISELY OR NOT, we make promises to children. By this I do not mean that we say, "We promise, on scout's honor, hand on the Bible, on my mother's grave, cross my heart and hope to die, etc., etc." Such expressions are but poor scaffolding to support a weak promise that cannot stand alone. Many of the children we serve have heard such words: I'm sorry, but I promise to be at your game next time; I promise next year I really will come to your end-of-year school party; I promise never again to forget your birthday. So, when a child in our Children's Enrichment Program asks one of our singers/storytellers, "Will you come back?" the answer is a clear and straight *Yes*. "I'll bet you are just saying that." Now what? The singers/storytellers show up. In time the child will trust an adult again.

Still, some say it is not wise to make promises to children. Why? Well, there are those who think the rules for promises do not apply when dealing with children. I recall hearing a grocer lie to a child who came to buy candy. When the child left, another customer asked, "Why did you lie to that child?" The grocer replied, "It's not lying if you are talking to a child." Others say it isn't wise because children are literalists: a Yes is Yes, a No is No. They don't realize that many adults build into their promise a lot of "ifs": if it doesn't rain; if I am not too tired; if I don't get a better offer.

Be that as it may, at the Center we make promises to the children. We say *Yes* and we show up. There is no substitute for showing up.

But a serious question is raised: how can you say *Yes* and show up when there is a big "if" in your program? The "if" is this: "if" we receive enough gifts, we will show up. An understandable "if" but not a real "if." You see, quite a number of you have addressed the "if" by giving scholarships for our Children's Enrichment Program ($140 each). Some have given two, three, as many as ten. We have been a bit lax in sending reminders when a scholarship is not fully paid or when a scholarship is not renewed. We will do better, promise.

But what if? What if? If there are not enough scholarships, do we say to the children, "We will be back if we get the money?" No; we will not say that. We will find a way to make our Yes a Yes. And how will that be?

Boiled peanuts, anyone?

(July)

MY WORLD JUST DOESN'T sound the same anymore. This sad fact hit me recently in a conversation with Sally, my neighbor's coon dog. She has for years blessed me with that deep, throaty howl of hers, late at night or in the darkness just before dawn. Look out, coons, here comes Sally! But not anymore.

I mentioned this to her when I went over to visit my neighbor. I didn't want to hurt her feelings but only to let her know how pleasant her voice had been. Contralto, I think. Not like the yapping of those little nine-ounce dogs carried in women's purses. "But you don't bark anymore," I said. "I'm a coon dog; bring me a coon and I will bark." She sounded a bit miffed. I got a little miffed myself. "Do you remember what a coon looks like?" "Of course I do," she snarled, showing both of her remaining teeth. I wanted to prove my point, so I rushed home, brought back an encyclopedia with pictures of animals, shoved it under her nose and said, "Show me which one is a coon." Sally rolled her sad eyes over the page and then confidently pointed to a giraffe. I didn't have the heart to tell her.

I miss the sound of Sally, but not only Sally. How long has it been since I heard the croaking of frogs in a small bog beside Maxwell Road near the railroad? How many seasons ago did I last hear the drumming of the grouse, the melancholy notes of the whippoorwill, the romantic call and response of the bobwhite? These are rural sounds; I am a rural person, why don't I hear them anymore?

But other sounds, too, are painfully gone: the church bell, the factory whistle at B.C. Jarrell and Co., the creaking rocker of mama's momma, the ticktock of the clock of daddy's daddy. And the train whistle. Oh, we have a train, and for it I am grateful. Daily it takes riders north to the Tennessee line, and about once a week it takes freight south to Marietta. It whistles at the Maxwell Road crossing and I whistle back. But it's not a choo-choo.

My world just doesn't sound the same anymore. But one sound is still here and will still be here until all sound is hushed. In fact, here at the Center we are dedicated to making sure this sound will always be heard: The sound of children laughing.

2010

WHEN TELLING STORIES it is not usually wise to respond to requests. However, when the request is thunderous (with me, it takes only two to thunder), I give in.

As a boy I spent pleasant summer evenings gathering fallen stars. As I think back on it, the spent stars were worthless, but it was something to do. My brothers and I would go into a field near the house, climb up on tree stumps (all that remained after the blight of a once beautiful chestnut grove), and wait for stars to fall. From these perches we could see exactly where they fell, and it was not uncommon to have the pockets filled within an hour. Sometimes, whether in greed or out of compassion for fallen stars that might otherwise go unnoticed, I do not know, we would sneak from the back porch with Grandma's clothes basket and harvest the remaining stars still flickering on the ground. And, sometimes, dragging the heavy basket home left us too tired to empty it. "We will do it in the morning," but in the morning Grandma was already fussing about a residue of gray ashes in her clothes basket. (Everyone knows you cannot save stars over until the next night.) We denied charges of having kindled a fire in her basket and snickered off to play, protected from punishment by the mystery. But during her last illness, Grandma called me to her bed and told me, almost secretively, that she knew what we had been doing with her basket. My guilty silence was broken by her instruction for me to bring to her from the bottom of an old chest a package wrapped in newspaper. I obeyed and then waited the eternity it took for her arthritic fingers to open the bundle. "Oh, it's gone," she said, showing me where it had been. In the bottom of the package, was a little residue of gray ashes. We stared at each other.

"You, too, Grandma? Why didn't you tell me?"

"I was afraid you would laugh at me. And why didn't you tell me?"

"I was afraid you would scold me."

A Taste of Milk & Honey

(September)

THE WAITING ROOM WAS FULL, but I was not anxious; I had an appointment. Still I felt the need to rush; the receptionist had said on the phone that an appointment does not guarantee a seat. But no worry—I'll take the seat of the next one in to see the doctor.

I signed in. Time of arrival: 8:15 a.m.; time of appointment: 9:00 a.m. I was number 14. I like to be in the 12–15 range. They say doctors hit their stride about number 12. Before that are the distracting chores: finding the white coat, washing hands, getting the stethoscope from the refrigerator, etc.

A nurse appears. "The doctor is running a bit late. Be patient." No problem. I brought reading material. I begin *War and Peace*. It is difficult to read standing. All are restless. A teenage patient asks, "Does everyone know *Kumbaya*?" The stares silence him. He must be in for a brain transplant. I finish *War and Peace* and begin *The Rise and Fall of the Roman Empire*. The man next to me is knitting. What is it? A sweater. It looked huge. For yourself? No, my mother. What a woman!

A nurse appears. "The doctor is running a bit late. Be patient." I stop at the restroom on my way down to my car to retrieve more reading material— *The Complete Works of William Shakespeare.* I return just in time to place my order; the patients are bringing in pizza.

A nurse appears. "As soon as I hear anything." Again to my car, this time for my shaving kit and a change of clothes. In my absence, the patients elect officers. I am now chair of the First Annual Reunion Committee.

A nurse appears. "The doctor is not coming in today. His doctor ordered bed rest. Maybe tomorrow." What? My doctor has a doctor! It never occurred to me: the doctor needs a doctor? Then if doctors need doctors, maybe parents need parents, maybe teachers need teachers, maybe pastors need pastors, maybe all helpers need helpers at sometime.

I'll be back tomorrow, and instead of one of my usual jabs ("running a bit late, aren't you, Doctor?"), I think I'll ask what I never asked before: "How are you feeling, Doctor?"

2010

(October)

A SCOTCH AGAINST THE COLD . . . that's what my father called the little pile of firewood gathered in the fall in anticipation of winter.

Actually, gathering firewood was a year-round chore because the cookstove was wood burning. The only other heating in the house was from a fireplace in the living room. And did it burn the wood! We dragged, chopped, sawed, and split, but it was never enough. We called on Lee Grant Graves, a neighbor, and he would lay in a back log that would not only burn for days but would also hold the fire overnight, making easier an early morning start. Once in a while the back log did not hold the fire, so Momma or one of us kids went to the Graves' home to borrow a few coals.

Our scotch against the cold was really much more than warmth; it was our family gathering place; it was fun, games, light, popcorn, and hot chocolate; it was a place to say "Good night."

Today, from my study window, I can see our scotch against the cold. It is two rows of wood, tall and wide and waiting for the chill. Nettie and I did not drag, saw, chop, or split; all that was done by good friends, Wendell and Jennifer Fox. That makes it all the more a comforting sight. We almost welcome winter. I say this knowing we have another source of heat, but sometimes that fails and we lay in a fire, and remember.

Not too far from here live children with no scotch against the cold. When the temperature dropped recently, I thought of them and knew that soon the telephone at the Center will bring calls for warmth. We have a small fund for responding to such calls, but it is by no means an adequate scotch against the cold.

If you want to help, write on your check "A Scotch Against the Cold." Stay warm.

(November)

I WAS SADDENED to learn recently of the Crystal Cathedral in California having to declare bankruptcy. My sadness does not come out of any personal connection with the church or its staff. I shared a platform on one occasion with the founding pastor. Nor am I of the same denomination. Nor am I privy to any of the causes for the fall into bankruptcy; they usually are many. I guess I became aware of my sadness when, in the televised report, a camera provided a view of members doing the cleaning and maintenance work and an overhead shot showed a near empty sanctuary on Sunday morning. An almost empty house of worship is always a painful sight, whenever, wherever, however.

Whatever happened to the Crystal Cathedral apparently came in the process of transition in leadership. Transitions can be awkward, painful, and untidy business, costly and hurtful for many; but not at The Craddock Center, for which I am more and more grateful every day. Evidences of a smooth transition are abundant: the Board is stronger and more active; the number of singers and storytellers for Head Start schools has increased; giving is up; the number of programs has multiplied; public awareness of what the Center is and what it does has grown; and most important of all, the Center remains true to its original purpose. If anyone who has been a donor to the Center has the slightest doubt about giving following the transition, let me assure you there is absolutely no room for uncertainty.

And how do you achieve such a transition? The answer is simple: find someone to be Executive Director who is more capable than the one leaving the post. We have done that.

God provides. . . . Boiled peanuts, anyone?

(December)

MY ONLY PROBLEM WITH SANTA CLAUS was that dadgum, good for nothing, plague take it (you can tell by my language I am still upset) list. Yes, the list. Granted, Santa knows when you've been sleeping, and he knows when you're awake, but his list is dead wrong. I don't care if he's checked it twice, he still does not know who's naughty and who's nice. I could have done a better job making the list. Let me be specific.

2010

I had a playmate who shot a red bird with a BB gun. What did he get for Christmas? A brand-new blue and white American Flyer bicycle. A neighbor boy never worked one day in the garden—not one day. What did he get? A real, live pony, dark brown with white stocking feet, that he named Stockings. Down the road lived a boy who played marbles for keeps, which everyone knows is the beginning of gambling. In spite of this criminal activity, he got a whole box of licorice that he didn't share with anyone. And his younger brother, barely old enough to talk, said the four-letter word for "the bad place." Santa rewarded his cussing with a bright red wagon with rubber-tired wheels. And did I mention his sister? Like all girls, she got away with everything, and in return she received a big doll whose eyes closed and which wet its pants.

And me? I'll tell you about me. I was faithful in Sunday School for two weeks before Christmas. I took my turn gathering eggs, feeding the hogs, and churning milk. I swept the porch before company arrived, and as Momma will tell you, I usually washed my hands before supper. I could go on. And what did it get me? An apple, an orange, some raisins still on the stem, a few walnuts, a stick of peppermint, a box of sparklers, and a little truck about six inches long that you had to push across the floor. That's it; you do the math. I don't care if he checked it twice or two hundred times, Santa's list was seriously flawed.

Or the whole system was. Naughty kids get nothing; nice kids get loads of good stuff—that's not the way life is. For instance, I know some beautiful children whose only sin is that they were born into poverty. And what will they get for Christmas?

That's up to you.

2011

(January/February)

WE WAITED OVER AN HOUR for the start of a meeting that never started. There were nine of us, we had no agenda, the conversation was random, the subject matter ranging from trivial to significant. But for some reason the vocabulary was limited. You might think that we had been so seduced by speed communication that we could no longer make full sentences. Single-word responses and short phrases abounded. And surprising, at least to me, was the frequency of the use of one word: issues. Listen to this: I have issues with my boss; I have issues with my daughter's friends; I have issues with the school system; I have issues with my doctor; I have issues with my heart, my kidneys, with my left knee, and on and on. How many times during that hour was "issues" used? A conservative estimate would be four million, six hundred eighty-three thousand, four hundred seventy-one.

I think I was the only one of the nine who did not use the word. And why not? I already had a word that functioned just as well, if not better, when you are talking but not wishing to say very much, at least not specifically. My word? Trouble. Some of you probably use it: I have heart trouble, stomach trouble, liver trouble, trouble with my neighbor, trouble with my knees, trouble with the church, the government, the school system, and on and on. It says enough but not too much, so why should I trade troubles for issues? If you already have troubles, who needs issues?

Now, I'm not saying I will never use the word. Very likely I will, but only if there is something at stake, only if there is a clear issue. For example, the children of the poor: who will see to it that they have a Head start, a Heart start, a Health start? I know that not everyone agrees that this is an issue. For some it is not even a trouble. I take care of my own children, so why should I feel any responsibility for someone else's children? Now I have trouble with that. No, I have issues with that view. Don't you?

If you do, will you please say so? One full sentence will suffice, attached, of course, to your check. Thanks.

(March)

I MUST ADMIT I was elated from the day of the phone call from New York until the morning the panel truck and automobile pulled into the parking lot of the church on the hill. *The New York Times* was preparing a program on "Religion in America" to be shown on the Discovery Channel. "Would you be willing to be interviewed on site? We would take no more than three hours of your time." I tried to sound cool, like this happens in Cherry Log all the time. A date was agreed on, and I waited.

The reporting team consisted of five young people, late twenties, early thirties, all very professional and most gracious. All from New York. Within minutes cameras, lights, and mikes were set up, tested, and declared ready. From the church we moved to the Center, and apart from a few shots of our beautiful mountains, my guests were satisfied and packed up as smoothly as they had set up. In slightly less than three hours, they rolled away. All conversed freely off camera, but only one engaged me in the interview. No, there was one exception. At one point in the interview, one of the group, a young woman, became quite emotional and asked for a break. I asked her if there was a problem and she said, "No; I just never knew that anyone was this deeply committed to their faith." She talked a while about her now-deceased grandparents, and then we returned to our work.

The young man conducting the interview was well prepared, asking good questions and capable in the spontaneous follow-up to the answers. He did, however, return again and again to one question: Are there any snake handlers around here? I first thought he was non-serious but I came finally to realize the matter was important to him. I said I witnessed snake handling in worship in Kentucky years ago, but that it was now against the law in every state except Virginia. But, he said, don't you think it is still going on? Probably, so I gave him the name of a preacher in the Church of God of Prophecy who would know.

Sure enough, when the program was on the Discovery Channel, the three-hour interview was about 40 minutes, and of that more time was given to snake handling than to any other feature of religion in Southern Appalachia. The reporter had found and filmed a snake-handling service. In fact, the reporter actually touched the rattlesnake, firmly held, of course, by the believer.

Oh, well, so much for religion in Southern Appalachia. But if I had known the reporter had such an appetite for a miracle, I would have taken him to a Head Start school and let him interview children in our Children's Enrichment Program. Talk about miracles. They are all over the floor!

(April)

"HIS HEAD IS FULL OF NOTIONS, but his heart is as empty as a churn." These are the words a mother used to describe her son.

Mary lived in a two-room, no-floor cabin on a mountain near Ozone. I was a student preacher in that area, and I took seriously Paul's example of ministering "publicly and from house to house." But Paul was a city preacher and I was in the country, some of it very remote. I had no car, but the loan of one enabled me to visit the widow Mary. "Is yours the only house on this road?" "No, there's one more on past me about half a mile." "Anyone live there?" "Yes, my son George." "Any family?" "No, he ain't never married." "Do you think he would let me visit him?" "Probably, but it wouldn't do no good, if you are meaning to talk to him about his soul." At this point she gave me the above description of him. Her evaluation of his condition should have prompted me to see George immediately, but it did not. Eventually, I went.

George's place was a picture of self-sufficiency: A lazy dog that hardly stirred, a dozen or so chickens in the yard, a small chicken house, a garden still bearing witness to last year's crop, and an outhouse. The house itself was apparently built by someone who didn't care. The front room contained a bed, two chairs, and a kerosene stove. In the other room was a woodstove, a small table, and one chair. A clutter of old newspapers surrounded the chair most worn. "It's clear you love to read," I said as I pointed to a wall full of shelves, and each shelf full of books. "I heard on the radio about them books. If you bought the whole set, they let you pay it off by the month. They're about half paid off." You could tell George was proud of those books. "I'm nigh on sixty years old and I ain't seen another set." The set was the Great Books of Western Civilization. Plato, Aristotle, Plutarch, Kant, Milton, Shakespeare, Dickens, Melville, Sandburg; you name it, it was there.

I didn't want to embarrass George, but I asked anyway, "Have you read any of them?" "All of them, some twicst." I listened as he talked fondly of what he had read. "Your favorite, George?" *"Plutarch's Lives."*

On a later visit, I asked, "Do you have a Bible, George?" "No, Momma does, but she don't like to loan it." On the next trip I took him a Bible and suggested he begin with Luke. On my last visit (I was moving away) I said, "George, what did you think about Jesus?" He looked down for quite a while and when he raised his head, I saw the tears. "I wish I could of knowed him," said George as he got up and walked outside.

(May)

"I AM FOUR," SHE SAID, as she held up three fingers. "She won't be four until July," said Beth, her mother. "I don't know why Debbie is so anxious to be four. Just the other day I overheard her say that when she was little she had to go to bed early, but now that she is four she can stay up as late as she wants to."

"I had a birthday recently." "And how old are you, Fred?" "I'm eighty-four," I said, as I held up three fingers. "He's only eighty-three," explained Nettie. "I don't know why he keeps lying about his age. He seems to think that a world of good things come your way when you are eighty-four. Maybe he thinks he will harvest a load of compliments, like are you really eighty-four; you look awfully young to be eighty-four. You don't look a day over eighty-three." Or maybe on Father's Day at church during fellowship time they will have a recognition of the oldest man present. You know how it works: will all the men seventy or older please stand? A host of men stand, but I'm not worried. Will all seventy-one or older remain standing. A few take their seats, looking defeated. Seventy-two? Seventy-three? Seventy-four? Seventy-five? They are dropping like flies. Seventy-six? Seventy-seven? Only eleven of us remain. Seventy-eight? Seventy-nine? Down go two more. Eighty? Two more drop. Eighty-one? Down go two more. I can smell victory. Eighty-two? Three more fall. Eighty-three? Another one, poor guy. Eighty-four? I look around; I am the last one standing! An attractive young woman (poor thing; she can't be a day over thirty) pins a red carnation on my lapel as I welcome the crescendo of applause from these young whippersnappers who have no clue what it is to achieve eighty-four.

But neither do I; I am only eighty-three. I must go and see Debbie and convince her that we simply must stop lying about our ages. Praise, falsely gained, leaves a bitter taste. If she is willing, I am ready to go public: Debbie and I are younger than we claimed to be.

(June)

NOTHING IS SO COMPLICATING, especially to a child, as finding one's self in possession of something not one's own. I do not have in mind those sibling disputes over a toy or the last biscuit or the last cookie. Those small dramas play themselves out rather quickly under the wise and caring eyes of our first referees, our parents. But set the complication in a larger arena and the matter, though in itself a trifle light as air, may go unresolved or resolved without satisfaction.

My earliest recollection of such a complication involved a baseball. I was nine or ten. Like many small towns, my hometown had a baseball team, and a good one, too. Semi-professional. Admission was ten cents, far beyond my budget. But the voice on the loudspeaker said to the boys outside the gate that anyone who wished to recover foul balls could present a ball to the gatekeeper and be admitted free. Chasing foul balls was a heated contest and not without scuffles. Finally, I retrieved one. When I presented the ball to the gatekeeper, he said the game was almost over. Why not hold onto it, and when the team returns in two weeks, bring the ball and you can see a whole game free. Nice man; I happily went home with the ball.

My happiness was short lived. From family and friends came questions: Where did you get the ball? Why didn't you return it? It's not really your ball, is it? What are you going to do with it for two weeks? Can we play with it until you return it? What if you lose it? What if it get damaged while you have it? If you don't show up with it, will the gatekeeper or even a policeman come to your house to get it? What's the good of having the ball if we can't play with it? I remind you this was a real baseball used by real ball players and nothing at all like the rags and string ball Momma had made for us. We guessed its value at a hundred dollars, or maybe five hundred.

The pleasure of holding the ball and letting my brothers and friends hold the ball soon wore off. Having the baseball gave me unwanted responsibility. And decisions; I had to make decisions. The next two weeks dragged on, with me fearful that something could go wrong; I could miss my rendezvous with the gatekeeper, and rumors about the ball could ruin my life.

Like I said, being entrusted with something not your own is a real complication. Especially for adults.

(July)

HOW WAS I TO KNOW that when the cows are lying down, the fish won't bite? This bit of information is vital, especially to an eight-year-old, the perfect age for fishing. I could not believe this knowledge was intentionally withheld from me, although I know for a fact that adults withhold information from children. How do I know? Walk into a room of adults talking and suddenly every voice is hushed. Why? You know. Or when a child lies ill in bed with a fever of 120° and an adult says, "Now run along outside and play," you know secrets are being kept.

Now that I think about it, most of the important knowledge I possess was gained by watching and overhearing. Nobody told me that if a snapping turtle bites you, it will not turn you loose until it thunders. Nobody told me that a dead snake hanged on a fence will continue to wiggle its tail until sundown. Nobody told me that you can tell if a watermelon is ripe by placing a broomstraw on the melon. If the straw turns a complete revolution, the melon is ripe. I picked up this information, nobody gave it to me. But it sure helps now and then when someone cares enough to just plain flat out tell you the truth.

So why didn't someone tell me that when the cows are lying down, the fish don't bite? We had a cow, for goodness sake! All those mornings I walked down to the farm pond with pole and worms, no one ever said, "Look at the cow on your way; if it is lying down, don't waste your time." Would that information have cost them anything? No. Would it have helped me? Yes, immensely.

It's not as if I was asking for an interpretation: did the fish get the cow to agree or was the whole thing the cow's idea? I don't care who started it or what the motive was. All I know is the basic information would have spared me many a disappointing day, the victim of a dark conspiracy.

Years later, my mother and I were driving out to the old farm where I was born. We passed a field in which were several cows, all lying down. "Not a good day to fish," she said. "You knew and didn't tell me!" My own mother; I couldn't believe it. She felt my pain. "You were just eight years old and you loved to fish. I didn't think *catching* fish was all that important. Besides, I did what I could." "And what was that?" "You remember Belle, our cow? Well, Belle promised me she would never lie down while you were fishing, and she didn't. I trusted her."

And so did I, and I trusted my mother, too. Trusting is very important, especially now, with all these conspiracies going around. Why, I heard the other day that cats can read your mind.

(August)

I PUT NO STOCK in the notion that whatever fragment of music or poetry is on the mind when one awakes in the morning is a harbinger of the kind of day it will be. I confess the experience is fairly common with me. I may be humming a hymn tune or a popular song, or I may be quoting to myself a line from Shakespeare or Milton or Sandburg. I may ask "where did that come from?" but I do not expect an answer. I do not go into the day with joy or dread dictated by this early humming or reciting. In fact, as the day wears on, the line or the tune will give way to matters of greater "pith and moment." It is over.

However, I must admit it isn't over if the humming or musing stops suddenly because I cannot recall the next line of the poem or the song. This failure to remember what comes next stalls the mind and gives to the fragment a longer life than it deserves. I give voice to my frustration and ask persons around me, "Do you remember the next line?"

That's what I'm doing now; I'm asking. I remember:

A snapdragon never snaps
No matter how it feels,
Except to try to catch a fly
To brighten up its meals.

I also remember the next line:

A dandelion never roars

and I'm stuck. My mind crashes at the end of the runway. Can you complete the stanza? I'm a proud man, but I'm begging for your help.

No, I'm not begging; I don't beg. I'm willing to bargain, so how about this? I've noticed over the years that generous people are also quite poetic, so if you recall those next three lines, just enclose them in the envelope with your gift and I have saved you 44 cents. Is that a deal or what? If you can't remember, just enclose a note to that effect along with your gift to the Center and you still save 44 cents. Same deal. If you can't remember but think you can write three lines just as good, enclose your poetry with your gift and you get the same deal: 44 cents saved. If you can't remember the three lines and can't compose your own, just send your gift without postage and we will rob our poor purse of 44 pennies to satisfy the postage due.

What a deal! Grace abounds!

(September)

THE WELL HAS BEEN THERE for as long as I can remember. It is situated about half way between our family home and town. Mr. Blakemore lived across the road from the well, but it was not his well. The family who owned it was long gone, their home had fallen in, only the chimney still standing.

The well now served as a public well, all thirsty passersby being refreshed by it. I drank from it, as did my family, our red mule, and Bess, our saddle mare. Since a Civil War battle had been fought nearby, I imagined the Blue and the Gray fighting over the well. And since the road led in the other direction into Crockett County, and into Alamo, the county seat, I had no doubt but that Ole Davy himself drank from the well.

The well was not like our well at home, which was open, water being drawn by a bucket, a rope, and a windlass. Rats and other varmints could fall into it, but not this well. It was closed at the top with a spout and a pump with a handle. Pumping the handle vigorously eight or ten times brought water to the surface and out the spout. Water was fresh and cool and free. No one claimed to own it, posting signs saying "Keep Out" or "No Trespassing" or "Whites Only." No one owned it, so everybody owned it and often lingered awhile exchanging news and gossiping. I loved that well and often stopped there when I wasn't really thirsty.

While it was true that no one made a claim to the well, the well made a claim on everyone who drank from it. A quart jar filled with water hung by a wire on the side of the pump. This water was not for drinking but for priming; that is, it was to be poured into the spout while you pumped. As soon as suction was created, water poured out. No matter how thirsty you were, first the jar was refilled, and then you drank. In other words, you prepared the well for the next traveler and then satisfied your own thirst.

But what if? What if you emptied the jar into the pump and it just didn't get primed? It could happen. Just to be sure of a drink, I could drink the water in the jar. Then what? Now the jar is dry, the pump is dry, and the next traveler is dry.

Please don't drink the priming water; I may be the next traveler.

(October)

It is interesting to observe, even in small children, the early signs of leadership ability. Of course, I am not referring to that bullying, pushing, shoving, "I must get my own way" behavior that, unless modified, carries over into adulthood. In adults it may be disguised, but it remains insecurity getting its own way, no longer pushing and shoving but now manipulating. Rather, I am referring to that "If we form a line, we will all eat sooner" or "Why don't we sit in a circle so we can all see?" leadership.

The quality of leadership not only appears early but it also is not necessarily joined to money or status or appearance. For example, a much beloved member of the community dies. All are in mourning and wringing their hands, but one sees that the lawn is mowed, pets are cared for, cars and drivers stand ready to meet planes, and a healthy meal is warmed. And the rest of us, no less sincere, are bringing in banana puddings, 37 of them. "If I had only known you were bringing one . . ."

When I taught in Oklahoma, I was a passenger on a train going from Kansas City to Oklahoma City. I was to exit at Perry, and I did, as did 90 other people. Due to heavy snowfall, the engine derailed in Perry. No one was hurt, but the announcement, "We will be here at least two days" was painful enough. Anger, crying, confusion, frustration, threats of lawsuits abounded, but in less than three hours, order prevailed. We were in an American Legion building, cots were coming in from the National Guard, refreshments with the promise of meals later came from churches, phones were provided.

How so? A cowboy was on the train, along with his horse. He rode his horse into the building and from the saddle he explained to us our behavior for the next two days: cots for those under eight, and those over 65 would be nearest the two restrooms; these two groups would be first in the food lines; a sign-up sheet would be near each of the four phones, no calls over five minutes, etc., etc., etc. None of us complained. Who was our leader? A rodeo cowboy. He had a gift for leadership.

At least "gift" is what the Apostle Paul called it, a "gift of leadership." In the church, he said there are gifts of healing, of teaching, of preaching, but also of leadership. Thank goodness!

While observing the children, I am encouraged. I hope they will not be deterred by adults who have the positions of leadership but not the gift.

(November)

WHEN I READ THE NOTICE of Henry's death, I was abundantly aware that I was now the last person living who knew How Alley Cats Got Started. If I am silent, I will be leaving large room for error, and who knows what will be told to the children. So please listen carefully; I will not speak of this again. Don't trust your memory; take notes. Ready?

How Did Alley Cats Get Started? Eleven-year-old Danny was given as a birthday present a cat from a rescue center. Not knowing the cat's birth name, Danny called her Phoebe. Lavished affection set Phoebe free from hostility and suspicion. She was an excellent pet.

One day Phoebe threw up on the carpet. Thinking she was seriously ill, a concerned Danny rushed her to the vet. The vet, a kind and caring old man, was busy so he told Danny to leave the cat and that he would call when Phoebe was ready to come home. The vet, bless his heart, was absentminded with serious memory loss. What did Danny say was wrong with the cat? Noticing that Phoebe's left ear was a bit shorter than the right, he said, Ah, that's the problem! He trimmed a half inch off the right ear, stitched it, and called Danny. Naturally Danny was upset, reminded the vet of the real problem, and left Phoebe there.

When the vet turned again to Phoebe, he scratched his head and pondered: What did Danny say was the problem? Noticing the length of Phoebe's tail and delighted to have found the problem, he removed three inches from Phoebe's tail, and called Danny.

Of course, Danny was furious. He explained again the problem, and this time wrote it down so the vet could not forget. By and by, the vet attended to Phoebe and asked himself, Now where did I put that note? His search was in vain, but he did notice Phoebe seemed hot in his un-air conditioned office. Cats with heavy fur need to be trimmed in the summer. Of course! Why did I not think of that sooner! Happily, he sheared Phoebe and called Danny.

Needless to say, Danny exploded. He spoke to Phoebe: I will leave you here overnight and tomorrow I will come and sit here while the vet attends to you. He will make no more mistakes. Hearing Danny's new plan, Phoebe jumped out the window, ran down the street, slipped into a dark alley and Danny never saw her again.

Now don't blame Phoebe; we would have done the same. Don't blame Danny; he wanted only the best for Phoebe. And don't blame the vet; he loved animals and would never intentionally harm any. Why look for someone to blame? Sometimes things happen, even painful things, and no one is to blame. That's the way life is. Right?

(December)

THIS IS THE SEASON when we are reminded that giving and receiving are one act, not two. Of course, for practical purposes we divide them. For example, there are times when it is important to stress that it is more blessed to give than to receive. At other times, attention is given to receiving. The church devotes four weeks (Advent) to prepare to receive the Christ child. But receiving without giving can be selfish, just as giving without receiving can be condescending. The New Testament understands this by offering one word for generosity (giving) and the same word for gratitude (receiving). That word is Grace.

I have a vivid memory of giving and receiving as one beautiful act. The occasion involved my late sister, Frieda. When her long battle with cancer was coming to a close, she sent word to friends to come by for a gift. Over the years she had received gifts from them: a vase, a wall hanging, a painting, silver tableware, and so on. When the friends arrived, she gave to each the gift that she had once received from that friend. I was stunned and embarrassed. We had been taught from childhood that you do not return gifts: you keep them, you prize them.

I stationed myself outside so that I could explain to the friends that Frieda was not ungrateful. This was so out of character for her. It must be the cancer or the medication. As the first friend came out of the house, I began my painful apology, only to be interrupted. "Oh, no; this is the most wonderful gift I have ever had. It is twice blessed; it has been both given and received. What could be more beautiful?"

Nothing.

2012

(January)

FOR THREE YEARS I have asked Santa Claus for a new Bible. I admit I did not try to make my case; I thought the gift made its own case. In fact, I was a bit proud of my request, thinking Santa would be relieved to have a break from assembling the very latest gizmos. Taking a Bible from the shelf of unrequested Holy Scriptures and blowing off the dust, he could sigh and say, "How long has it been!" But no, instead I received a tie with a note, "Hope you still like wide ties." What happened?

Maybe I do need to make my case, so the next year I did just that. I don't mean I tried to justify the gift by giving Santa a list of my merits, impressive as that would have been (the very thought puts a strain on my humility). If Santa has a list and has checked it twice, then surely I deserve a Bible, for crying out loud. So I attached to my request a brief description: New Revised Standard Version, large print. As if he didn't know of my recent eye problems, I explained my request for a Bible in modestly enlarged print for public reading of texts for the day.

I faced Christmas with confidence, only to be disappointed. Santa's note was a reprimand. "Now, after 65 years of preaching and teaching, you are wanting a Bible. A bit late, don't you think? Enjoy your socks."

You may now be saying to yourself, "Forget Santa Claus; go buy yourself a Bible." Easier said than done. In the first place, buying and selling, for goodness sake! I have never bought a Bible; every Bible I have was given to me. Giving and receiving, not buying and selling, seems

104

more fitting. But even if I decided to buy one, where do I go? You would think a Christian bookstore would be the place. I called around; plenty of Bibles but no NRSV. "We carry only the true Word," one voice said. OK, so I am going to a regular bookstore, they have all kinds of Bibles. But I dread it. I can hear the clerks now: "Well, if this isn't a shocker! After all these years explaining the Bible, and now you are going to read it. This confirms some people's suspicions, Fred. May we put this on Facebook?"

Does this mean Santa didn't give me a Bible this year? I don't know; I haven't gotten up the nerve to open my gift. It still lies under the tree. Judging from the package, it could be, but I hope Santa didn't include one of those notes.

(February)

ONCE THE COURT DETERMINED that the differences between the two parties were not reconcilable, rulings were made to implement as fairly as possible separate existences. Most noticeable was the division of property. One group was allowed to continue use of the building, the other was given land and resources to build their own. So now there are two churches where there had been one.

But, surprisingly, to passersby there was still only one. If you were driving south toward Dayton and Chattanooga, off to the right you could see a white church building with two steeples. However, if you stopped and drove a quarter mile toward the church, you would see not one with two steeples but two churches, each with one steeple. One was an exact replica of the other, with no more than eight feet between. The one difference was in their signs, one inviting you to First Church of Walnut Grove, the other to The Original Church of Walnut Grove. Thus they continued, quarreling and dwindling, for less than four years. Unable to survive financially, both churches closed. Today, one of the buildings is gone; the other, minus the steeple, is a hay barn.

Occasionally traveling in that area, I inquired about the rift that eventually killed the church, or should I say, the churches. I guessed, since the place was near Dayton, that the Scopes Trial of 1925 that pitted William Jennings Bryan against Clarence Darrow (creation vs. evolution) may have split the church. Not so. Power struggle between two families, said some. Inspiration of Scripture, said others. Suspicion of embezzling church funds, was one answer. Disagreement over the choice of a hymnal, several had heard. The dismissal of a pastor with a wayward eye, not a few whispered. So what is the truth?

None of the above. The truth is the division arose over fellowship meals. Oh, they were abundant enough and frequent enough and delicious enough. That is, until Pastor Newman came. Pastor Newman ate only Cheerios. Only Cheerios! Breakfast, lunch, dinner. At the church? He brought his own. In your home? He brought his own. It was maddening! What did Mrs. White whose peach pies were to die for think about it? What did the church men who fixed a huge breakfast every month think about it? We're insulted! We will fix him; at church and in our homes we'll serve only Cheerios. No, thanks; he brought his own. Word spread in the community; the church was a joke. Pastor Newman had to go. Without taking time to look up Cheerios in the Bible, the church board fired him. But it was too late; everything was now a matter of dispute. From bad to worse to worst, whatever the subject.

Finally, there was no alternative; they would have to go to court.

(March)

I THINK IT BEST THAT I GO AHEAD and turn myself in. Mind you, it is no easy decision. I talked with three lawyers to get an opinion about my chances in court. All three laughed: vagrancy is hardly a charge that will get you on a court docket. But doesn't Georgia have vagrancy laws? Yes, but they are antiquated at best, in the same category as not installing a bathtub on the second floor or not grazing a cow on the front lawn on Sunday. What in the world gave you the idea that you were a vagrant?

Well, I looked up "vagrancy" in the dictionary and found that vagrancy "is the state of being a vagrant." Wow! How could we live without the dictionary? But the dictionary went on to give equivalent words: wanderer, vagabond, tramp, nomad, wayfarer. And "pilgrim." I like that: I am a pilgrim. My ancestors were pilgrims; I proudly speak of the Pilgrim Fathers. My faith tells me I am: "This world is not my home, I'm just passing through."

But is "pilgrim" not simply a religious disguise for "vagrant"? Religion is often used, not to change us but to hide who we are. How did Shakespeare say it? "There is no error so gross but what some sober brow will bless it with a proper text." It is time to come clean: I am a vagrant. And so are most of my friends. They prefer to call it "retired," but it is all the same. Are you from around here? No. That's what I thought. And I suppose you have no job? No. Where are you going? Nowhere; I'm just out walking. Do you know anything about recent crimes in this area? What crimes? May I see your identification?

You know the routine. You are, and you are seen as, a vagrant. But no problem. Lazy maybe. Shiftless maybe. No visible means of support. No plans for the day. No rush; been there, done that. Relaxed. I sleep well at night and fairly well in the morning, but in the afternoon I just toss and turn. May see a doctor, but then again I may not. But the community and the church locate me, and I am no longer simply a vagrant; I am "a person of interest." The camel's nose is in the tent. The person of interest is soon charged and convicted of the oldest crime on record: "akedia," "I don't care." This downward spiral is fatal.

I suggest you turn yourself in.

(April)

ON MY DESK ARE three items that seem to be unrelated to each other and to my work as a teacher and preacher: a stick of wood, a piece of string, and a small stone. But the fact is, since I was five years old I have possessed a stick, a string, and a stone, and they have always been magic. It is pleasant to remember the times they have saved my life as sword, or lasso, or deadly missile. When I had all three in my pockets, I walked safe and proud among tigers, gangsters, and outlaws. When there was no danger around, I sat on the porch just to watch myself walk by.

It has not been necessary for me always to have the same stick, string, and stone. It is necessary only that they be magic. The stick now on my desk is about 14 inches long, about 2 inches in diameter, and round. Both ends and the sides bear the teeth marks of a beaver. I picked it up in a grove of young poplar trees near Hemptown Creek. The string came to me from a box of books shipped from Chamblee to our new home in Cherry Log. And the stone caught my eye in the bed of the creek running beneath our home. But where is the magic?

I was given a leave from Emory to complete a textbook on preaching. I spent most of the time in a cabin on Hemptown Creek. During the writing (all my writing has been with pen and paper, just as the Bible says we should do), my hands became dysfunctional. I spoke of it with colleagues, and I consulted physicians. But most importantly, I called on the stick, the string, and the stone for magic. Their instruction was clear and simple: I tied one end of the string around the middle of the stick and the other around the stone. Then with both hands on the stick and with arms outstretched, I turned the stick until the stone was at eye level. I reversed the process and then repeated it five times. My arms were tired, my fingers were tired, but quicker than a wink, the agility of my fingers was restored and I was writing again.

I don't see how anyone can write a book without believing in magic. Oh, some try but before you read a dozen pages, you yawn and lay it aside. No magic.

(May)

THE QUESTION WAS ASKED by a TV reporter and directed to Carl Sandburg, poet, historian, biographer, storyteller. The question was, "Mr. Sandburg, what in your opinion is the ugliest word in the English language?" I was interested because I grew up with "ugly words." My mother's list of ugly words included taking God's name in vain, cursing, swearing, and using profanity. These words were not to be spoken. Also not to be spoken were words not ugly but close enough to come under the ban: darn, heck, gosh, etc. Also not to be spoken were eleven words that sounded alike but in reality were different. For example, "But, Momma, I was saying dam, not damn." This long list of ugly words came back to mind when the reporter asked, "What is the ugliest word?"

Through the years, as I have outgrown my mother's list (at least, some of them), I have added to my own. For example, "ilk." It is an old Scottish word meaning "like, or the same." "The drug dealers and their ilk," or "the tax collectors and their ilk." Ilk is ugly, real ugly.

But I silenced my mind; Mr. Sandburg was about to speak. I grew more anxious as he grew more deliberate. Finally: "The ugliest word in the English language is *exclusive*." He said no more; he did not explain his choice or attempt to justify it. His face said it all—what could be uglier? I tossed my boyhood list—how childish! I tossed ilk and all its ilk—how useless! On a slip of paper I wrote "exclusive." I dared not speak it lest my tongue cleave to the roof of my mouth. As I sit here years later I can hardly say the word, it is so ugly. And when I think the word, I feel I should wash my mind out with soap.

(June)

FOR THE LIFE OF ME I can't tell you a thing the speaker said, being as I was totally consumed by the distraction in the seat beside me. The room was filled with preachers, men and women, and I felt myself fortunate to find a seat, the speaker being of such reputation. But had I known the person beside me, I daresay I would have stood in the back of the room.

It is difficult even now to convey to you the nature of the distraction. It was a noise, not loud but constant, much like the ticking of a clock, and it came from the person beside me. However, he gave no evidence that he himself heard it. At first the sound was bewildering: what is it? A medical device to sustain failing lungs or a weakened heart? Or a cell phone, or a smart phone, or a stupid phone? I went beyond bewilderment; I was infuriated.

Can't you turn that thing off?

No.

Why not?

At intermission, he explained. "About three months ago I was honored by an invitation to preach in a prestigious church. I prepared in my usual way, but with greater intensity: study of the biblical text; theological reflection; study of the expected audience; search for analogies in literature, in history, in current news; attention to movement of the message; reading great literature to keep the imagination alive; and prayer throughout. I was as ready as I could get. Three days before the date of delivery, I was suddenly and seriously ill. On the appointed day, I was flat on my back."

"Do you know what it's like," he said, "to carry around an unpreached sermon, continually ticking, ready to detonate but unable to do so? I almost envy those preachers who prepare generic sermons, to whom it may concern, one size fits all. If one's schedule is interrupted, no problem; preach the sermon the next Sunday. But I can't do that. We've known since Aristotle that a key to effective communication is appropriateness: this message is for this audience, on this date, for this occasion, for this purpose."

The intermission ended. "Do you preach regularly?" "Yes," he said, "I am the pastor of a congregation."

I wonder if that congregation realizes what an extraordinary preacher they have. Surely they do.

2012

(July)

PERHAPS YOU HEARD the government has decided to stop minting pennies? Has a date been set? I don't know, but I do know that date will be a dark one, indeed. Just thinking about it brings in melancholy like a fog.

Mind you, I will not lash out at the U.S. Treasury; those poor dubs wake up every morning and go to bed every night with endless reminders of million dollar, billion dollar, trillion dollar debts. What then is a penny? A penny is so nothing it's pitiful. Nor will I wallow in fond memories of Depression pennies. You know the routine: "When I was your age, a penny would buy a stick of licorice."

All I ask is that they think about it. The penny is our most stable coin. A penny is one *cent*, a *cent* meaning a hundred, as in *century*. One hundred cents equal a dollar. We know how unstable the dollar is, but not the penny. Come Depression, come Inflation, it doesn't matter; on any day go into a bank, hand the teller a dollar, ask for pennies, and you will receive one hundred—every time! Why not wise up and convert all your money into pennies?

But the issue is not really money; the issue is our way of life, our culture, our language, our music. Take away the penny and out go penny loafers, twenty penny nails, pennies from heaven, penny-pinchers, penny-ante, penny-wise and pound-foolish, a pretty penny, pennyweight, and a penny for your thoughts. And where would you buy your clothes, at J.C. Nickels? But not to worry: the irrepressible penny is here to stay. Even if the government not only stops minting them but calls in all the pennies out there promising 10 cents for each one, will we all turn them in? No. Some, yes; that dime for a penny can be awfully tempting, but some of us will not, cannot. You see, pennies are our friends, and you cannot turn in your friends.

But fret not; all this will blow over like an empty threat and across the country children and adults alike will bend over, smile, and say, "Look! A penny; this is my lucky day!" And it is. Look carefully at it. It says

United States of America; one cent; the date minted; Liberty; *e pluribus unum* (out of many, one); In God We Trust. And it bears the images of the Jefferson Memorial and the head of Lincoln. I am proud to say that I have in my possession five pennies.

I even have an Indian Head penny. Ever see one? Priceless.

(August)

I AM RESIGNING from the Millard Fillmore Society. This may come as a shock to some of you, so let me explain.

The Society is named for Millard Fillmore, 13th President of the United States. His years in office were 1850-53. As you can see, he held the office less than one term, having moved from Vice President to President upon the death of President Zachary Taylor. I became a member of the Society by virtue of my family's move from Ramona Drive to Fillmore Street in Enid, Oklahoma. I did not know of the Society until after the move. Membership in the Society was not a motive in the move, but I must acknowledge a slight feeling of upward mobility at the time.

We had been in the house on Fillmore about four weeks when I received a card welcoming me as the newest member of the Millard Fillmore Society. The card informed me that the sole purpose of the Society was to meet annually to discuss and to celebrate the achievements of Fillmore's presidency. I would be notified of the time and place of the next meeting. There were no dues (obviously the Society was endowed). The next spring I received a card stating that there would be no meeting that year, the president having forgotten the date. The following spring a card came stating that there would be no meeting that year and for the same reason. And so this notice continued for the two years we were in that house, and it continues to the present day, the card being forwarded to my Georgia address. The move to another state did not invalidate my membership.

At first this "know nothing, do nothing" Society suited me quite well; I had commitments aplenty. A fellow can get spread too thin. But I eventually felt guilty, thinking perhaps retaining my membership was depriving some deserving soul who might covet a place on the roster. I mailed my resignation to the address on the card, but my letter was returned, stamped by the post office, "No such address exists."

I suppose I am still a member. If you are not too busy already, I would be glad for you to be my guest at the next meeting. I'll let you know the time and place.

I'll drive; no problem.

(September)

I HAD ABSOLUTELY NO INTEREST in buying a car when I drove into the lot where dozens of used (pre-owned) cars were on display. My purpose was to do the owner a favor. Let me explain.

Every day between home and work, I passed this car lot. These "like new" automobiles were shown to the public with their prices in large letters on the windshields. From time to time the cars were moved around, with the exception of one car. Always in a favored spot was a real eye-catcher, an Olds Cutlass Supreme, a canary yellow convertible with black interior. Price: $300. Must be some mistake; one zero omitted, but even at $3,000 it looked like a real steal.

One day it occurred to me that some buyer would see the mistake and offer the $300 to the horrified but helpless owner. I drove in to warn the owner of the mistake so he could prevent a huge loss. But he said there was not a mistake, $300 was the price. It can't be; what's wrong with it? I kicked the tires, checked the odometer (165 miles), searched for evidences of being wrecked or flooded, turned on the ignition and listened. It hummed like a hive of bees. Okay, what's the catch?

This car does have one unusual feature: it will take you not where you want to go but where you ought to go. Really? Yes. How many owners? One. Do you have his phone number? Yes. I called and verified the strange truth about the car. What is it like to have a car like that? Absolutely horrible, he said. One Saturday I missed my tee time because I was at a nursing home visiting with the residents. One evening I missed dinner with friends because I was ringing the Salvation Army bell for three hours in front of Macy's. I recall a Sunday when my wife was away, I drove down the street to get a paper and a six-pack and that crazy car took me to church and Blessed Assurance.

I noticed the other day that the car is still on the lot. The price has been marked down to $30.

Interested?

(October)

WHEN THE OLD DOG DIES the proper protocol is to wait a season of remembering before acquiring another. Shorten the season of remembering and some might question your love for the old dog, while others of darker minds might whisper suspicions of your already having an eye on the next dog. Nothing could have been farther from the truth. He told me more than once that he did not intend to get another dog, not now, not later, not ever.

You can imagine my surprise when I stopped by and he answered the door holding a pup. I was stunned but said nothing. He felt the need to explain and did so. A friend, one of those who seem always to know better than you what you really need, brought a pup. No explanation was offered; the friend knew a puppy sells itself.

How old is the pup?

Six weeks.

I always thought eight weeks was weaning age, but what's done is done. The puppy was cute; they always are. It was white and black, more white than black, without pattern.

What kind is it?

Part fox terrier, part beagle, part dachshund, part Boston bull and maybe a little fice.

I laughed at the genealogy. Well, the American Kennel Club won't be giving you papers on this mix. I know, and I certainly won't be asking for any. His reply puzzled me. He explained that papers are given to prove that your dog is exactly like every other one of its breed! This pup is not like any other in the world. It will be unique in appearance, in personality, in habits, in bark. I can't wait to see how it turns out.

I never thought of mixes that way.

Is it male or female?

Male.

Does he have a name yet?

Yes. His name is Maude.

(November)

REMIND ME LATER to tell you the story that was on the tip of my tongue when Trisha told me she was retiring as Executive Director of The Craddock Center. Her announcement did not kill my story, but it did postpone it.

We will deal with our loss and her move into a well-earned future during these next few months. Just now I want to thank her for a job extraordinarily well done and to wish her joy in the anticipation of the next chapter of her life. And to you, our readers and supporters, I want to say four things:

First, we are in a strong position to move into the future. The Board is at its strongest, the Center gains new friends every week, and our staff is more talented and more dedicated than we could ever have imagined.

Secondly, it is already apparent that there will be no shortage of applications for the position of Executive Director. It will be a matter of finding the best among the good.

Thirdly, our mission and purpose will not waver one iota as we move into the future, confident of the continuing favor of God.

Finally, when we begin to interview candidates, we will remind each of them of the two words at the heart of all we do: ***Happy*** and ***Hope***. Even when we look on faces that bring tears to the eyes of God, we will bring Joy and Delight and eyes bright with Hope. And God will smile too.

(December)

SOMEONE WITHIN THE SOUND OF MY VOICE will respond in a very personal way to our search for a new Executive Director for The Craddock Center.

Maybe I said that poorly. We have already had many responses that were personal: expressions of regret over the loss of Trisha by retirement; prayers for our continued growth under new leadership; promises of continued financial support through this transition; offers of increased giving, dispelling any fear of program loss during this change. All these are personal responses, to be sure.

But I am thinking of a response more intensely personal. Suppose you receive the news of our search and you have the feeling that the news did not go out to everyone but only to you. And you cannot shake the feeling. You try to distance yourself from it: exactly where is Cherry Log? What is The Craddock Center anyway? I could empty my pockets for these poor children but what else could I do? Could I ever be so bold as to ask others for financial support? And how does one enlist all those volunteers? The present staff and Board of the Center seem to find in the poor children of Appalachia their reason for getting up in the morning. Am I capable of such passion? One gets the feeling that the search committee believes that out there somewhere is someone called to this work. You might say that.

These are exciting days around the Center. Our mission remains the same, but something or someone new waits around the corner.

Grace to you, and peace.

116

2013

THERE IS A PLACE in the Austrian Alps where one can stand, shout out "Hello" and have the word return fivefold. It is as though the hills join in chorus to welcome you. And *five* times: Hello, Hello, Hello, Hello, Hello. No sound is quite so cheerful and warming as an echoed Hello.

But there is in North Georgia a place where one can stand, shout out "Welcome" and have the word return, not five times, not ten times, not fifty times, but countless times. The Alps are so imposing and grand that one almost expects an answer to one's greeting. By comparison the Southern Appalachians are small. Beautiful, yes, but the hills are older, the lakes are smaller, and the forests have suffered more from axe and saw. But set your feet on the right spot, turn your back to the breeze, lift your eyes to the horizon, fill your lungs with a warm Welcome, and it will happen: "Welcome." Don't stand there thinking the Welcome will end soon; it will not.

The Place I have in mind is in Cherry Log. Soon now I will take Julie Jabaley, our new Executive Director, to the Place. When she is positioned properly, I will, without fanfare or explanation, speak to the lakes, the hills, the forests, one word: "Welcome." Look at Julie's face as all creation in chorus greets her: "Welcome." Wave after wave comes the echo, "Welcome."

I have things to do, so I will leave her there. She also has things to do, but not now.

(March)

I WILL CONFESS THAT I was only half-listening as the news reporter ran through a list of programs that would be affected if the Compulsory Budget Cuts went into effect. But I was alert enough to be jolted when I heard "Head Start." Surely not! This program has brought life and light and hope for thousands of poor preschoolers. No one claims that the program is without flaws, but the Center has worked closely with these schools for over ten years and we know a good investment in children when we see it.

Then came the second jolt: "Speaking of shortages," said the reporter, "we have learned that the inventory of drugs used in the execution of criminals in Georgia is alarmingly low." Apparently two drugs are joined in order to be lethal, with a third drug that reduces pain and anxiety being available on request.

Can you believe it? A civilized and sophisticated society with a system in place to eliminate the unwanted being so inattentive to be able to kill only a half-dozen without begging or borrowing from another state that is ready and willing? This is serious; political heads must roll.

But out of the embarrassment will come quick solution: now that the budget cuts have crippled the Head Start program, surely that program can limp along on a few dollars less. With the promise to pay back the borrowed money, several vials of the lethal drugs can be rushed to Jackson and everybody can relax. We are all safe. After all, what could be more *unnerving* than having a cage of criminals still alive when they were supposed to be dead last month? In fact, other criminals still on the loose, upon hearing of the drug shortage, might be emboldened to go on a crime spree. And that calls for more police officers, more squad cars, more courts, and more jails, which means, of course, more taxes. If you look closely you may recognize among the new criminals several boys and girls who missed out on getting a Head Start because the school was closed for lack of funds.

(April)

I AM NEVER READY for the question even though I know he will ask it, the "he" being my physician and the question being "Have you fallen since your last appointment?" But this time I was totally not ready because he did not ask me; rather he redirected the question to Nettie (I no longer drive to Atlanta): "Has he fallen since his last appointment?"

Like the plague I hate that maneuver! Don't you? The doctor talks to someone else about you while you sit there in plain sight, treated like a deaf mute. Surely there is a chapter in the medical manual entitled, "Talk *to* the patient, not *about* the patient when the patient is sitting in front of you."

But my pain lies deeper: the good doctor apparently does not like the answers I gave when he asked me the question on previous visits. I thought my answers were more than adequate, well researched and presented with clarity and focus. For example, since I knew he knew that I had taught in a theological school, I thought a theological answer would be appropriate. Beginning with Genesis and Adam and Eve, I traced through the Bible "fall" as a metaphor for the human condition, lacing my response with bits of Coleridge and Milton, quoting Arthur Miller's *After the Fall*, and closing with a modest commendation of God borrowed from St. Jude, "Now to him who is able to keep you from falling."

In anticipation of the question during today's visit, I prepared a response drawn from sociopsychological interpretations of Adam and "the fall." When one falls in public, that moment when down on all fours recalls one's kinship with our animal ancestors. And what is that immediate glance around us to see if anyone saw us fall but an acknowledgment of human vulnerability? Such is the nature of a fall.

I was ready for the question, "Have you fallen since your last appointment?" But the question was directed to Nettie and not to me: "Has he fallen since his last appointment?" I was hurt, yes, but I was nervous for her, the question being unexpected and therefore without a prepared response. "Yes, Doctor, once," she replied. "I was running the vacuum in

the hallway, I left it to answer the phone, and he tripped over the hose."
Poor Nettie, clearly unprepared! That was not a vacuum hose in the
hallway. In the dim glow of a night-light, I saw it move; yes, move. It was
the serpent, the serpent of the Garden of Eden, and I am back in Genesis.
I couldn't believe that the doctor seemed satisfied with her answer. I wish
he had asked me. Doesn't anybody read the Bible anymore?

(May)

WHEN I ACCEPTED the position of Corresponding Secretary for the
Southeastern Division of the American Vocabulary Association, it never
occurred to me that the exercise of my office would involve so much pain.
Of course, I anticipated some sadness and disappointment when perfectly
healthy words would suffer abuse by overuse. As you know, I have spoken
and written about such degeneration of our vocabulary as one finds in the
common practice of using the same word to cover a multitude of actions
and emotions. I offer as an example the word "issues." "I have issues
with" hardly says anything specifically about floods, barking dogs, dull
sermons, or high prices. Such generalizations fill the empty speech of
groundlings who have neither eye nor ear for the world around them.

Let us, as members of the Vocabulary Association, resolve here and
now to be more specific in our speech. But the pain I have in mind comes
from the apathy with which some of our members respond to the deaths
of perfectly good words. As you know, we hold big memorial services for
words that pass away. Last month I sent notices RSVP to all our members
urging attendance at the memorial service in Pikeville marking the passing
of our old friend "Against," as in "It cools off against the sunsets" or "I'll
be ready against you get back." The burial of this beloved word should have
drawn a crowd. But how many came? Three, and they shed no tears.

I am now sending notices of the demise of a word that died from
neglect. I haven't heard it used in over forty years. I expect a few protesters
will be present, insisting that the word is not dead. They will wail at the

grave, claiming deep affection for the word although they never use it. Maybe their noise will shake us awake and make us realize how really few good words we have left. If you are planning to be in Greenville for the service, may I ask you to come prepared to say a sentence or two using this remarkable word, sending all of us home with new zeal to pass along to our children our priceless vocabulary?

The word? The word is "ilk."

(June)

I LEARNED LONG AGO that when two checkout lanes are open, that the other lane is moving faster is an illusion. Accept that illusion as reality, pull out of your lane, move into the "faster" lane, look back at your previous lane, and it will be obvious that your previous lane is moving faster than your present lane. Don't change lanes! I can't explain it; farther along we'll understand why.

But my lane was not moving at all, stalled by a dispute between the cashier and a young customer standing before a mountain of groceries insisting that the check on Chip and Judy's Family Bank of Fargo is a real check on a real bank. Nobody budges; the manager is called over the intercom; I'll never get out of here.

A break! The manager moves my line over to a counter previously closed, a clerk appears and we're in business. I am customer number 3. I am busy rechecking the dates on my purchases; it has been a long time. Customer 1 moves through without incident, but customer 2 has a problem. Let me break it down for you; I know, I was there.

A young woman, a fretting child in her arms and a small girl at her side, was paying for the modest pile of potatoes, cabbage, beans, etc. "So you are on food stamps?" "Yes, ma'am," she almost whispered, obviously not wanting the fact to be a public announcement, which it now was. "And how are you going to pay for *these*?" asked the loud clerk, picking up a small bundle of three red carnations. Before the young mother could answer, the clerk announced, "These are *food* stamps. You can't buy flowers with food stamps. What were you going to do, eat them? Hardly a day passes by that somebody doesn't try to buy beer, or cigarettes, or lottery tickets, or flowers with food stamps."

The young mother sank into embarrassed silence and turned to walk away. Several in line offered to pay for the flowers. She refused. "I've been shamed enough already. Them flowers has turned to weeds now. It's just that this is my little girl's birthday and she loves flowers, especially red ones."

Outside an old man waited for them. I lingered long enough to hear him say, "Didn't you get baby doll no flowers? Then we'll just go down to Mrs. Shepherd's. She raises flowers, lots of them, and she will be more than happy to give you an armload, and they'll be prettier than those old store-bought ones."

I can't get this episode out of my mind. It needs to be fixed. Can you fix it?

(July)

THERE WAS A TIME and not too long ago, when airports across the country were hospitality houses. Not only were we welcome to use their facilities to come and to go, but friends and family of travelers were also welcome to gather for heartfelt Hellos and long Goodbyes. Cameras flashed, gifts were exchanged, promises were made. And these scenes were not curbside, but in the waiting areas for arriving and departing flights. In fact, it was not uncommon for a relative or friend to board the plane to help the traveler "get settled in." Visiting continued until the announcement that "All persons on board who do not have a ticket to Kansas City must now exit the plane; we leave in two minutes." I recall seeing 14 Mennonites weeping their way off a plane, leaving behind a teenage girl sitting alone with a basket of fried chicken, still warm and smelling very, very good.

But it is not so now. If you must say Hello or Goodbye to someone, say it at the curb as the car slows down, not stopping, of course; this is a No Parking zone. The fine is $50. Nobody likes this new world filled with hatred, suspicion, and hostility, but it is what it is. The fried chicken has to be confiscated; we can't be sure it is chicken.

But now and then my memory reaches behind these dangerous days and I recall passing time waiting on my flight, looking at those gathered at the gate and making guesses: On whom are they waiting? To whom are they flying? Some of my guesses were wide of the mark, I am sure, but not all. Some, in fact, were easy. The clues were too many and too clear. That young woman over there, staring at the gate, checking her watch constantly, going repeatedly to the counter to inquire if the flight is late. Very attractive: cheerleader type. She is wearing a jacket, much too large, "Yellow Jackets" across the back. No more mystery; she is a cheerleader at Georgia Tech and she is waiting on her boyfriend, probably the team captain. That huge ring held on her small finger with a roll of adhesive tape, that is his ring.

The plane arrives and after an eternity, passengers pour out, many at first, then a few, then none, then a few. No team captain. She is frantic, then rushes to the door, bending over a frail, elderly woman in a wheelchair. She takes the chair from the flight attendant. "I'll drive," she said. "Grandma, I was getting worried, but you are finally here. Hang on, we have a million things to do and tons of talking." And then to those of us nearby, "She's really my great-grandma. She's 94. Doesn't she look terrific?"

Okay, so I guessed wrong. But I'm glad.

(August)

I WANT IT TO BE UNDERSTOOD at the outset that my quarrel is not with all birds; certainly not. Were we talking about birds in general, I think I would clearly come down on the side of admiration and enjoyment. In fact, I would go so far as to say that my relationship with birds as a lot is therapeutic. For example, the blue heron that comes fishing crawfish and small trout in the stream that runs beneath my house has provided conversation at dull tables at which I would otherwise have nothing to say. Or again, during my long illness I occupied myself for hours observing how birds move when not flying. Some hop, some run, some walk, and some hardly move at all except to fly.

Having spoken favorably of birds in general, I must add that individual birds have on occasion won my admiration for acts of courage against cats and snakes and acts of sacrificial love when caring for their young.

Even so, nothing said thus far settles or even soothes the quarrel I referred to at the outset. That quarrel is with the Eastern Phoebe. This bird comes in numbers, multiplies through one or two nestings, and moves on. The Eastern Phoebe is welcome; those that are truthful will tell you that. The several feeding places testify to my hospitality, as do the numerous birdhouses. There are eight or ten of these houses, different colors, different sizes, and different locations. But now this little drama turns ugly. The Eastern Phoebe has yet to visit one of the feeding places. Too proud? I don't know. Prefers bugs? I don't know. And in 18 years not once has the Eastern Phoebe occupied one of the houses. The Blackcap Chickadee has, and happily so. The Bluebird has, leaving Thank You notes. But the Eastern Phoebe—nada. I don't want to be peevish, but I think I deserve an explanation.

Then one day we almost came to blows. I put up one more birdhouse. It was special to me. It was a gift from colleagues on the occasion of my first retirement. It was folk art, the sides made of re-used wood and the roof of rusted metal. However, most striking was its shape: a country churchhouse, steeple and all. How could the Eastern Phoebe resist it? I could hardly wait.

The next morning Mr. Phoebe was waiting for me at the back door. "This is a new low, even for you. You tried to lure me with brightly colored 'cages' you called houses. That failed, so now you play the religion card. A cage that looks like a church is still a cage. No, thanks!"

Where did I go wrong?

(September)

MY **HEART WAS NOT IN IT,** but I went anyway to see a clocksmith. I did not need a clockmaker; I have clocks. I have one floor clock, two wall clocks, and two mantel clocks. To be honest, I may have only one wall clock since I don't know how or where this one clock was attached to the ship in Queen Victoria's fleet. Maybe I shouldn't count it at all since it did not strike or chime, but rather tolled the duty hours for the sailors.

At any rate, the ship's clock was now silent, in need of repair, as did they all. Well, that is not exactly true. One mantel clock, inherited from my grandfather, still works when I wind it, but I often forget. You see, it is a twenty-four-hour clock, but why should I give it daily attention when the others will go three or eight days on a single wind? But now they are all silent, in need of attention from a clocksmith. At first I welcomed the silence, but soon felt ridiculous, a houseful of clocks and not a single strike or chime. Friends raised questions. I had to see a clocksmith.

I went reluctantly; I'm not sure why. Mine was the reluctance appropriate to entering a sanctuary, quiet and humble and certainly without any intention of intruding. And why not with reverence? A clocksmith among his clocks is a wise man wrestling with the central question of our lives: What time is it? It is as though the sun and moon had whispered the answer and the clocksmith has tried to express it with his clocks. I am not trying to get all spooky on you, but you will have to agree that it would be inappropriate to burst into a clocksmith shop munching on French fries and slurping a giant coke. Remember that you are entering another world, a world of wisdom born of memory, and this old man among his clocks just might change your life.

I hiked my body into motion toward the clocksmith's shop. Soon I stood before his door, steadying myself to ask the question that will begin or end the conversation: "Do you make house calls?" Once inside I was met by a young woman, mid-thirties, and welcoming. "The clocksmith's daughter," I assumed. "Is the clocksmith in?" "I am the clocksmith," she said. At that moment an old feeling rolled over me, the same one I experienced when Rev. Mary came to be our pastor, the same one I experienced when Dr. Kathy removed my appendix. "I'm sure you can help me, but give me a few days." "Of course," she smiled, "some things take time."

A Note from the Editor

You know you've been reading great stories when the end leaves you wanting more! And the work of The Craddock Center has not yet reached the point where we can say, "Happily ever after!" about the folks we serve.

Yes, these stories—and the work of The Craddock Center—are "to be continued." And right about now, I am hearing Dr. Craddock's voice, "As I was saying . . ."

So, for your next Fred B. Craddock story, please see the next edition of *Milk & Honey* in your mailbox or in your inbox. You might just clip it and paste it at the end of this book, and you'll have a head start on *More Tastes of Milk & Honey*.

We haven't heard the last of that boiled peanut stand!